BAD BLOOD

CASEY SHERMAN

BLOOD

Freedom and Death
in the White Mountains

University Press of New England

Hanover and London

Published by

UNIVERSITY PRESS OF NEW ENGLAND

One Court Street, Lebanon NH 03766

www.upne.com

© 2009 by University Press of New England

Printed in the United States of America

5 4 3

Library of Congress Cataloging-in-Publication Data
Sherman, Casey, 1969–
Bad blood: freedom and death in the White Mountains /
Casey Sherman.
    p. cm.
Includes bibliographical references and index.
ISBN 978-1-58465-679-1 (hardcover)
1. Vendetta—New Hampshire—Franconia—History.
2. Violence—New Hampshire—Franconia—History—
20th century. 3. Kenney, Liko d. 2007. 4. McKay,
Norman Bruce, 1958–2007. I. Title.
HV6452.N18.S54   2009
364.152'3092—dc22   2009024888

University Press of New England is a member of the
Green Press Initiative. The paper used in this book meets
their minimum requirement for recycled paper.

For the people of Franconia

Contents

*Illustrations follow
page 102*

BAD BLOOD

Prologue

September 2, 1994

It was my first day on the job and I was completely overwhelmed. I had just been promoted from production assistant to news writer for the morning news at WHDH television in Boston. I was only a year removed from college and I was faced with one of the biggest stories of the year. Just a few hours into my shift, police scanners blasted an alert that a Massachusetts State Trooper had been shot on the job on Route 3 in Kingston, thirty-six miles south of Boston near Plymouth. We didn't have a name, and we didn't know the severity of the trooper's injuries, but we did know that we had to react immediately. The executive producer sat down with the assignment editor and formulated a plan; within minutes I saw reporters running through the newsroom with photographers lugging heavy equipment close behind. They all jumped into a fleet of news vehicles and satellite vans and spread out. Some correspondents headed directly to the scene, while others fanned out to area hospitals, making sure we would be covered in case either the unnamed trooper or the shooter was brought in for treatment. As the morning wore on, we continued to gather tidbits of information as to exactly what had happened on that stretch of highway south of Boston. The trooper we found out was thirty-one-year-old Mark S. Charbonnier, an eight-year veteran of the Massachusetts State Police. Trooper Charbonnier was newly married and working on his law degree at the New England School of Law. We also learned that Charbonnier and the suspect had each been shot four times during what was supposed to be a routine traffic stop. The gunman, David Clark had been carrying two pistols, two ski masks, a screwdriver, leather gloves, and a police badge in his red Chevy van. Clark was also a convicted killer out on parole who knew he'd be sent back to prison for the curious items in his van. Clark apparently figured it would be easier to murder a state trooper than to explain the burglary tools to a judge. David Clark survived the shooting, while Mark Charbonnier did not. At trial, Anne Marie Charbonnier, the trooper's widow, called Clark an "untamed animal who needed to be put down." This case was considered cut-and-dried, black-and-white. Trooper Charbonnier was a called a hero for taking the bullets that eventually would have been fired at someone else, given Clark's violent history. David Clark was sent off to Walpole State Prison, never to be heard from again. The mad dog wasn't put down, but chances are that he'll never see the outside of a prison wall. Sadly, the story repeated itself again and again over the next several years. The lead characters had all changed, but the scenarios were mostly the same. In each instance, you had a courageous police officer shot down by one of the untamed animals of the world.

The script was dramatically altered on May 11, 2007, on a quiet country road in Franconia, New Hampshire. I was working at another television station, WBZ in Boston, when the call "Officer down" came screaming over the police scanners on the assignment desk, a glass-enclosed pod in the middle of the newsroom. The call kicked off a flurry of activity as the assignment editor quickly calculated the drive time between Boston and Franconia, while the producer got the graphics department working on a map of the shooting scene, in case we needed to get on the air immediately and break into prime-time programming. There is a shared sense of excitement and dread working in a newsroom in full crisis mode. The instant adrenaline rush allows you to focus on covering the story, while in the back of your mind, you're thinking about the Anne Marie Charbonniers of the world, wives and children whose lives had been torn apart by one man's cold, cruel decision to pull the trigger. From the untimely death of JFK, Jr., to the unspeakable horrors of 9/11, I'd found myself on the front lines of countless breaking news stories, but on this evening, I was more spectator than active participant. My shift had long been over, and I was hanging around the WBZ newsroom catching up on some paperwork. As my colleagues had things under control and didn't appear to need my help, I began thinking about what the next few days would bring. If the speculation was correct, and the officer had died in the line of duty, there would no doubt be a massive public funeral attended by fellow police officers from across the nation. I could visualize the dramatic scene of the flag-draped coffin and the tearful remembrances. As for the gunman, there were unconfirmed reports that he too had been killed. I was a bit relieved that his death would spare the officer's family the emotional burden of a long, drawn-out criminal trial. I was also somewhat confident the killer would eventually be forgotten as just one more untamed animal in a criminal subculture full of them. I was dead wrong.

May 3, 2003

It happened sometime late at night or early morning. Despite what must have been a deafening roar, no one had heard a sound. There were no witnesses. Many had been predicting his downfall for generations; still, his death came as a shock to all those who knew him. There was no foul play involved, the cause they said, was natural: old age. He was about ten thousand years old after all. Others would argue that we all had played a role in his demise. His remains had been discovered the next morning by two employees while out conducting a routine inspection of the park. Later that day, his immediate family, the people of Franconia, New Hampshire, gathered in the drizzle and fog to see what was left. There was nothing. The symbol of their community, their state, their way of life was lost forever.

The Old Man of the Mountain had stood sentry over Franconia Notch long before the first real man had ever set foot here deep in the Pemigewasset wilderness. The notch itself covers about six miles with Franconia Ridge on the eastern border and Cannon Mountain to the west. The ridge is comprised of Mount Lafayette (5,249 feet), Mount Lincoln (5,108 feet), Mount Liberty (5,108 feet) and Little Haystack Mountain (4,460 feet). It's an area popular with day hikers; roughly one-third of the trail is above tree line, offering up some of the most breathtaking views in New England. It can also be quite treacherous, with trouble spots like "The Knife's Edge" and "Dead Ass Corner" (the latter getting its name from a mule that fell to its death after being spooked by lightning). As dramatic a site as the Franconia Ridge is, it doesn't hold the same aura as its wayward brother to the west. At 4,100 feet, Cannon Mountain is a bit smaller, but it also had a rock formation jutting out from its southern crest that appeared to have been carved by God himself. In reality, the Old Man had been formed by glaciers into five red Conway granite ledges some twenty-five feet wide and forty feet high. With his furrowed brow, prominent nose, sullen mouth, and sharp-pointed chin, his was not a kind and comforting face. His was a New Hampshire face. The Old Man's unforgiving profile was both a welcome and a warning to those seeking freedom and adventure here in the North Country. Daniel Webster made note of this in one of his most famous oratories. "Men hang out their signs indicative of their respective trades," Webster wrote. "Shoe makers hang out a gigantic shoe, jewelers a Monster watch, and the dentist hangs out a gold tooth; but up in the Mountains of New Hampshire, God Almighty has hung out a sign to show that there *He* makes men" (in Mudge, *Old Man's Reader*).

Webster was not the only learned man to marvel at this nearly mystical natural wonder. The Old Man had also been mentioned by Longfellow in his signature poem *Hiawatha*. In his short story "The Great Stone Face," Nathaniel Hawthorne called the Old Man, "a work of Nature in her mood of majestic playfulness." With apologies to Hawthorne, *playful* is not a word that immediately comes to mind when describing the Old Man and his importance to the region. According to one local legend, members of the Mohawk Indian tribe worshipped the Old Man and believed it to be their god Manitou. "When a band of Mohawk warriors had burned and massacred down below and had been driven back by the Pennacooks, they returned up the long winding Notch trail and exhausted slept through the night," Pulitzer Prize–winning author Ernest Poole wrote in his 1946 book, *The Great White Hills of New Hampshire*. "At sunrise they spied that great face frowning on them from the clouds. 'It is the Manitou!' they cried. As they fell on their faces, darkness came, and out of thunder and lightning they heard the Manitou say: 'You have made war on your brothers and your hands are stained with blood! You have dared to enter this place of the Great Spirit unsummoned, and the penalty is death!' As they lay trembling on the ground, lulled by a strange spellbinding song, they fell asleep and turned to stone and became the boulders found there still" (in Mudge, *Old Man's Reader*).

Another fable suggested the Old Man was actually the Indian God Ulala who had climbed Cannon Mountain to witness the retreat of the local tribe from the encroaching white man. It was said that Ulala's tears rolled down the mountainside forming the lake beneath. The first white settlers to discover the Old Man were Francis Whitcomb and Luke Brooks, while both were working on the Notch Road in 1805. They noticed it while washing their hands in the lake at the base of Cannon Mountain. "That is Jefferson!" they exclaimed, referring to Thomas Jefferson who was president of the United States at the time. Soon after, others began calling it "The Old Man" or "The Profile." Word about the natural wonder continued to spread and sightseers flocked to the area by stage-coach, paying as much as seven dollars for a first-class seat. Hotels also began sprouting up in Franconia Notch, catering to the grow-ing tourist trade. Signs of wear were first noted in the 1870s when a group from the Appalachian Mountain Club discovered that a large boulder in the Old Man's forehead appeared to be loose and in danger of falling off. No action was taken at the time. It wasn't until 1916 that a quarry manager, or "scenic surgeon" from Quincy, Massachusetts, traveled to Franconia Notch and installed three sets of 450-pound anchor irons to keep the boulder in place.

The area was preserved as a state park in 1928 and the Old Man became New Hampshire's official state emblem in 1945. During this time, the New Hampshire Department of Public Works and Highways began construction of Interstate 93 through Franconia Notch. The highway brought millions of new visitors to the area, but it also hastened the rock formation's downfall. The Old Man's caretakers were worried that vibrations from the blasting and road construction could cause its granite ledges to shift position. Their concern was not unfounded. In 1954, a geological study conducted by the University of New Hampshire found that the crevice at the top of the Old Man's head had widened nearly an inch over the past seventeen years. Three-quarters of an inch does not appear to be that significant a distance until you realize the slab of granite that had moved weighed more than three hundred tons. New Hampshire's leaders felt the need to save face, literally. They could not allow the state symbol to fall victim to a massive rock slide. Measures were immediately taken and workers covered the crevice with a wire fiberglass canopy. More important, four massive turnbuckles were installed to hold the loose boulders in place and a strong epoxy was used to seal a number of cracks lining the Old Man's weathered face. Despite the geological face-lift, some experts believed the Old Man was living on borrowed time. As far back as thirty years ago, state materials and research engineer Paul S. Otis said, "Natural forces are at work against the Old Man, and I'm afraid they will eventually emerge victorious."

Otis's sentiments, however, were not shared by the Old Man's longtime caretaker, Niels F. F. Neilsen, Jr., who said decades later, in 1999, "My gut feeling is that any baby born on this date, today, will not see the Old Man come down." Neilsen first laid eyes on the great stone face while visiting the area with his fiancée in 1947. He returned a decade later and landed a job with the New Hampshire Public Works and Highway Department, eventually joining the crew responsible for the Old Man's upkeep. "I had sailed around the world several times as a merchant seaman, and I had never seen anything like him," Neilsen once told reporters. "I don't believe anyone can be up there, even for one trip, and not . . . be awed at the . . . handiwork [that went into] taking a pile of rocks and shaping them into a great profile." Neilsen died in 2001, his ashes buried in the Old Man's left eye. Just a couple of years after that, the Old Man itself met with a similar fate. On a dreary Saturday in May 2003, the people of Franconia and the surrounding communities showed up to pay their respects. Some came alone, others with family and friends. Mourners laid down flowers, cards, and even a walking stick for the Old Man's next journey. A few even cried for the Old Man as if they had just lost a cherished member of the family—and in some ways, they had. What they had lost was a shared sense of identity. It's what New Yorkers would feel if the Statue of Liberty were violently knocked off her perch. It's what Arizonans would feel if they woke up to see that the Grand Canyon had suddenly been filled in. To the people of New Hampshire, the state emblem and the state motto are one in the same: *Live Free or Die*. This defiant pledge is emblazoned on the hearts of all those who call this rugged land home. It's what drew Liko Kenney's family here three generations ago. It is also what lured a police officer named Bruce McKay and a troubled ex-Marine named Greg Floyd to Franconia Notch.

He was not a killer, but it wasn't hard
for him to whip that .45 Hi-Point out.
It was in him somewhere.
JOHN "BILL" KENNEY

Franconia, New Hampshire
May 11, 2007

The lush lupines were waking from their winter slumber and the budding cone-shaped lavender perennials were a sign that spring had finally arrived here in the North Country and, more important, that summer was just around the corner. The locals call it "spring foliage" and they celebrate the lupines' arrival with a three-week festival each June. Unlike the bright red, orange, and yellow leaves that set the countryside ablaze with color each autumn, the lupines create a more tranquil tone, illuminating the rolling landscape with soft pink, purple, and white hues. The lupines grow wild here in the White Mountains, thriving despite the odds and the elements. Lupines are the ultimate floral survivor, sprouting up each year from the harsh granite-laden soil. Liko Kenney also considered himself to be a survivor. He had finally made it through the winter living alone in his parents' rustic cabin just off Easton Road. Some friends and relatives didn't think he could do it, but, much like the lupines, he had proved them wrong. He knew a great deal about wildflowers; many thought of Liko as something of a wildflower himself. Liko, whose name in Hawaiian means "bud," had been around gardens his whole life. That's why his new job fit had him so perfectly. Liko had spent the past three weeks working at Merrill's Agway in nearby Littleton, just two exits north of Franconia on Interstate 93. The rewards for a job well done were sore hands, an aching back, and sometimes even a smile from the boss. This was honest work here in the North Country, where men and even some women chose not to hide their callused hands, but instead displayed them proudly. Liko's boss, Don Merrill, was a friend of the family who had decided to take Liko on as a favor with the full knowledge that the twenty-four-year-old Patrick Swayze look-alike with long brown hair often tied back in a ponytail had a reputation of being "difficult." Don Merrill, however, a short and barrel-chested man who did not suffer fools easily, saw no signs of Liko's wild spirit during their brief working relationship. "He had a reputation as being bad, unbridled," Merrill remembers. "But he was a hard worker. Sure, he was opinionated, but he was also a lot of fun to be around. The kid was good for business." Liko Kenney had given Merrill a ride in his 1984 Toyota Celica earlier that day. "He drove me to pick up my truck. I was getting a new tire. Liko was excited to give me a ride. He was so damn proud of his car," Merrill smiles. The pleasant memory fades quickly as he looks down at the floor inside his sparse office. "I never saw the gun."

Liko Kenney liked to drive fast, much faster than the 45 mph he was going right now. He was still over the speed limit, but conservatively so. The frost heaves were settling from the previous winter but the road was still riddled with bumps and divots. The uneven surface could wreak havoc on any vehicle, especially the car Liko was driving. He fought the urge to put the pedal to the metal for two reasons. He wanted to protect his twenty-three-year-old car and he also didn't want to get pulled over by the cops—perhaps because the registration had recently expired on his Celica, or because he had a pot pipe in his car along with a film canister filled with marijuana seeds. Smoking pot was not frowned upon by his family; in fact, it had always been encouraged. The Kenneys were a clan of hippies, after all, and they had always butted heads with local law enforcement. But none more so than Liko. He knew that his light-blue Supra coupe was a target for police. He had told friends that he was saving his money to move out west, far away from the White Mountains of New Hampshire and far away from the police officers he felt had been harassing him for years and pushing him toward the edge. Some called him paranoid, but they hadn't been walking in his shoes over the past month. He was still licking his wounds from the trial that hadn't gone his way. He also had the unnerving and unshakable feeling that he was being followed. The .45 Hi-Point semi-automatic pistol that he kept under his driver's seat had given him plenty of problems in the past, but it also helped ease his mind.

Liko tried to remain upbeat around his passenger and friend, Caleb Macaulay. The two had just finished a tough nine-hour day of work at Merrill's Agway. Liko had spent much of the day in the warehouse, loading mulch into cars and trucks and answering customer questions like, "Which is the best potting soil to use?" while Caleb had spent his time planting tarragon and other herbs in the greenhouse. The peaceful setting mirrored the young man's personality. Unlike the outgoing, sometimes fiery Liko, Caleb was both quiet and shy with timid, fawnlike eyes that complimented his dark features. "I love my job," he would tell investigators later. "I'm in greenhouses all day; I get to think about stuff. I work around people but I don't always have to *be* around them." Caleb was the timid puppy to Liko's alpha dog. Their personalities were poles apart, but that may also have been the secret to their lifelong friendship. Caleb was planning to follow his pal out west to Oregon, if he could only keep Liko out of trouble long enough to make the trip. Caleb was delaying the pursuit of his own dreams so that Liko could chase his. Liko Kenney's dream was simple: freedom. Freedom from his enemies, both real and imagined, and freedom from his own family, who he felt had always treated him as an outsider. Caleb's desires were more focused. He had recently been accepted to a massage therapy school in Boston. He figured this career path would allow him to make his own hours; in addition, it would keep his own body and mind healthy. Caleb felt that working with his hands at Agway was good training for his career as a masseur.

The exotic smell of massage oil was surely more enticing than the odor of dirt and sweat that permeated Liko's Toyota Celica as the two men drove along Route 116, headed for Liko's place to make Jell-O shots with the half-gallon of Smirnoff Raspberry Vodka and cranberry juice that they had purchased at the state liquor store in Littleton and at Mac's Market in downtown Franconia. The booze would help take the edge off. Maybe they'd call some friends over for a little party. After all, Liko had the house to himself for the next few days, until his parents were due back from their small coffee farm in Hawaii. Caleb had been staying with Liko while his parents were out of town, but so far it had been no bachelor's paradise. It had been a long twenty-four hours for the two young men; much of the previous evening had been spent chasing down several of Liko's pet hens and roosters after the birds had escaped from their pen during a thunderstorm. That night ended with their enjoying a couple of beers on the couch, watching *The Simpsons* before passing out from exhaustion. This night would be different. Liko and Caleb would get their second wind and make the most of it.

They were heading southbound on Easton Road by the airport, which was nothing more than a rural airstrip that offered soaring glider rides over Cannon Mountain to the public. Then they passed a white SUV with blue lights on the roof and the words FRANCONIA POLICE stenciled along the side. Liko took his foot off the gas pedal and immediately applied the brake, slowing the Toyota Celica down to about 35 mph. The stretch of road curved right and Liko lost sight of the SUV. Locals refer to it as Dead Man's Curve, although no one is sure whether anyone has actually died there (a friend of Liko's was involved in a head-on crash around the turn that had left him paralyzed a few years before). Liko took the corner slow and then exhaled. He thought he had slowed down just enough to avoid the officer's attention. His hopes were dashed a few seconds later when the SUV came into view with its siren wailing and blue lights flashing. Liko didn't stop right away; instead, he kept driving. The Toyota traveled another hundred yards or so before Liko spotted a turn-about on the right hand side and pulled in. The police SUV came in right after him.

Liko gazed into the rearview mirror as the officer stepped out of the vehicle. It was *him*. It had always been *him*.

Franconia Police Corporal Norman Bruce McKay, "Bruce" to his friends, had recognized the Toyota Celica right away as it sped past him on Route 116. McKay was fair-haired, clean-cut and had a reputation of being no-nonsense. "A real hard ass," some towns-people would say. He knew that Liko Kenney was behind the wheel and he knew that Liko's registration had expired. To some, this could have been seen as a minor infraction, but there were no minor infractions so far as McKay was concerned. The officer reported it to dispatch and said he was about to initiate a stop of the vehicle. "I'll be out with New Hampshire passenger 1961215," McKay radioed in referring to Liko's license plate number. "It's gonna be on Route 116 Franconia and if you have a Sugar Hill unit available, I'm gonna have an operator as Liko Kenney and he's gonna have a partner with him."

"Where on 116 are you?" the dispatcher asked.

"Approaching the intersection with Coppermine Road," McKay answered. "That'll be a registration shows expired four of 2007."

Sergeant David Wentworth of the nearby Sugar Hill Police Department heard the call come in and thought, *oh shit*. He was fully aware there was a river of bad blood flowing between Bruce McKay and Liko Kenney. Wentworth was sitting in the passenger seat of his cruiser alongside patrolman Phillip Blanchard. "Be advised we're on the back side of Pearl Lake Road, we are headed that way," Wentworth informed the dispatcher.

"10-5, be advised he has an operator with a passenger," the dispatcher replied. "I did not catch the name, he must be familiar."

"Yah, I caught the name," Wentworth answered. "And I'm familiar." The veteran cop explained McKay and Liko Kenney's turbulent history to Phillip Blanchard as they began making their way toward Easton Road.

★ "License and registration please," McKay demanded, staring down at the driver through the tinted lenses of his wire rim sunglasses.

"Why are you pulling me over?" Liko asked, with more than a trace of agitation in his voice. He rolled up his window, leaving it open only a crack. The window served as a symbolic barrier between the kid and the cop.

McKay offered no explanation. "License and registration please," he repeated. "Please shut the car off."

Liko refused to comply. "Sir, can I have a different officer interrogating me or asking me this?"

Corporal Bruce McKay shook his head. "No, you're pretty much stuck with me."

Liko persisted, "I would really like another officer here."

"You don't make that choice," McKay shot back.

Liko reached for his Nokia Trac Fone and frantically dialed a number. "What are you doing? Who are you calling?" Caleb whispered from the passenger seat. Macaulay saw fear in his friend's eyes for the first time. Liko didn't respond. He made three quick phone calls but could not reach anyone.

Frustrated and scared, Liko's next move came as a shock to his buddy. Liko grabbed the stick shift, put the Toyota Celica in gear and tore off with tires spinning leaving behind a deep set of tracks in the dirt.

★ "Liko was territorial," Bill Kenney tells me a full ten months later. "He's an earth sign, a Taurus. He's gotta have his way. That's very important, ya know." We are sitting across from each other inside his small cabin on the grounds of the Tamarack Tennis Camp just across the Franconia town line in Easton. The dwelling is one of six scattered around the vast 460-acre property. It's got indoor plumbing and gas heat for cooking and bathing, but not much else. The cabin is just more than thirty years old, but it looks a century older. You step into it and you step back in time. It's naturalist-chic, a place where Henry David Thoreau would have been content to hang his hat. Its spruce bones were pulled from the deep forest surrounding it, the logs then cut down and nailed together with mill wood to form the two-story structure. Inside, there is a cramped kitchen area where Kenney's Kyrgyzstanian wife Larisa, whom he met through a Web site several years ago, tries to look busy and stay out of her husband's way. It's a difficult task in a room as small as this one. The tiny kitchen opens to an equally small and sparse living area. There is no soft couch on which to sit or any other creature comforts for that matter. There's only a plain wooden table and two chairs, one of which he offers me. The cabin is quite warm on this late winter day and the smell of the wood-burning stove invades the nostrils the moment you enter. Bill Kenney calls himself a "gentleman farmer," but he's the closest thing to Jeremiah Johnson that I've ever seen. He's a mountain man, to be sure, but he's a pioneer of choice and not necessity. The former prep school kid and Middlebury College dropout is tied to the land not for financial reasons, but because of a deep emotional connection. South of the tennis camp, trees are being cleared and million-dollar log cabins are getting built at a steady pace. Bill Kenney would never dream of selling his property. Tamarack is home.

Not that he could sell even if he wanted to. The land is currently tied up in a family trust that has created a bitter divide over property rights among him, his sister Jo, and two surviving brothers, Mike and Davey. Another brother, Peter (Bubba as he was known) died when he was twenty-five. In a family full of wild ones, he was *the* wild one. Bubba had been a member of the Middlebury College ski team and an all-around talented athlete. He was considered by many as the prince of the Kenney clan, but he also showed a complete disregard for his personal safety, time and time again engaging in death-defying stunts like diving head-first off bridges without checking to see how shallow the water was below. Fate eventually caught up with him during an early spring kayaking trip on the icy waters of Franconia's Echo Lake. The skies were clear when Bubba left Tamarack with a red plastic kayak strapped to the roof of his white Toyota early that morning. The weather changed quickly once he was on the lake. The temperature plummeted as heavy rain and strong winds whipped through Franconia Notch. The first sign of trouble came from the camp's head counselor, who said there was talk in town about a kayak being found on the shore of the lake. Family members rushed down to Echo Lake to see if it was their beloved Bubba. It was. Bubba's kayak had flipped over, leaving him trapped in the bone-chilling water. He drowned within a few short minutes. Divers found his body a short time later. The tragic loss continues to hang heavy over the family today.

During the first few minutes of our interview, Bill Kenney says nothing. I can feel him sizing me up with that familiar Kenney stare. His intense blue eyes radiate both intelligence and defiance, a trademark of the entire Kenney clan. It's the same look his other renegade nephew, world-class ski champion Bode Miller, uses to thumb his nose at the sport's stodgy establishment who claim he's too undisciplined and too much of a maverick to be the ambassador of American skiing. Bode Miller says he never wanted to be an ambassador of the sport or anything but what he is: the fastest downhill skier in the world. Miller quit the U.S. ski team in 2007, deciding instead to go it alone. The decision proved to be the right one a year later in 2008 when Miller won his second overall Alpine Skiing World Cup title in four years. Bill Kenney has been accustomed to answering questions about his famous and sometimes petulant nephew. Answering questions about Liko is a relatively new phenomenon, one that Bill Kenney doesn't appear all that comfortable with. Like other family members, Bill had had his own problems with his nephew, whom he refers to as "the Polynesian." The uncle pulls gently on his long, untamed gray beard and gazes out a cabin window covered by frost. "He considered all this Liko Kenney's sovereign nation," he says with a sad laugh. "He went up to a local official one time and told her that all the land from 116 to the top of the Kinsman Trail was Liko Kenney's sovereign nation. That's an example of his extreme behavior. But he wasn't an extreme killer. He was just extreme in every other way."

"Where are you going?" Caleb Macaulay asked in a full panic.

"Caleb, I'm just trying to go to my uncle's house so there's witnesses," Liko replied, never taking his eyes off the road.

Macaulay knew this wasn't the right course of action. "Liko, this isn't gonna . . . I mean taking off after you were just sorta gonna get a speeding violation by a guy that already doesn't like you too much. You're pretty much screwing yourself."

Liko Kenney didn't have have time to argue. He kept driving. *Gotta get to Tamarack, gotta get to Tamarack,* he thought to himself. For him, the town line and the Tamarack Tennis Camp were his salvation. Liko may have seen himself as Ichabod Crane in Washington Irving's classic short story "The Legend of Sleepy Hollow." He just had to make it over the town line, as Crane just had to make it across that bridge near the Old Dutch Church to escape the Headless Horseman. His eyes darted from the road to the rearview mirror and back to the road again. Corporal Bruce McKay's SUV was following close behind. They passed the Kinsman Lodge where Officer McKay's vehicle suddenly lurched forward, passing the Celica on the lefthand side. Bruce McKay then stopped in the middle of Route 116, threw the SUV in reverse and turned the vehicle hard to the left, boxing the Celica in and prohibiting Liko Kenney from traveling any further. McKay kept turning until his SUV was directly facing the headlights of Liko's 1984 Toyota Celica. *I've got you now,* McKay must have thought at the time.

Liko Kenney and Bruce McKay had been antagonists for years, ever since their first violent encounter at Fox Hill, where Liko grabbed the officer's testicles while resisting arrest. The physical pain from the incident was long gone, but the humiliation was a never-ending torment. The officer hated the young hippie, but he also knew how dangerous Liko Kenney could be. Just two weeks prior, McKay had typed up the following warning to his fellow police officers:

Officer Safety Notice
Subject — Liko Kenney, 128 Easton Valley Rd, Easton NH
On April 24th 2007 the New Hampshire State Police prosecuted Liko Kenney in Littleton District Court for the assault on his [juvenile] cousin. The cousin and [the boy's] grandmother served witness against Kenney, the State won its case and Kenney was found guilty. After the trial while still in the court room, Kenny approached [the victim and his grandmother] demanding they pay his fine. State Police recommended to the [family] that they not pay his fine and Kenney left the court with the fine unpaid [status of the fine is unknown].

Prior to trial it was reported that on at least three prior occasions Kenney attempted to influence [the witnesses] not to show for trial as, *"bad things may happen if you do."*

Following the conclusion of the trial Kenney was visibly upset with the court, police and [the witnesses], who have since left the state for unknown period of time as they fear for their safety.

As a result New Hampshire State Police Troop F circulated an e-mail to their troopers advising of the potential for volatility should contact be made with Kenney in unrelated matters as there remains an open investigation at Troop F concerning Kenney.

On April 25th 2007 two photographs were taken of the entrance way to the Kenney residence as it appeared Kenney had intentionally parked his vehicle in a manner that would block the drive and access to the residence.

Kenney is known to own a .45 cal semi auto hand gun and a blow gun with steel shafted darts. Kenney has both a drug history and a history of resisting arrest or detention.

This notice is for informational purposes only in the event an officer finds them self [*sic*] working an incident involving Kenney. There is no current wants or warrants for Kenney at this time.

> Date of Notice 04/25/07
> Cpl Bruce McKay
> Reporting

Bruce McKay clearly understood the potential risks involved in dealing with an unpredictable young man like Liko Kenney. The officer had even taken the time to warn others that Kenney had owned a gun. So why didn't he heed his own warning and proceed with caution? McKay appears to have been blinded by rage. He was angry that Liko Kenney was trying to make him look ridiculous *again*. They were two opposing forces, and neither appeared willing to back down.

Liko Kenney's Toyota Celica now sat nose to nose with McKay's SUV. He stuck his left arm out the driver's side window and pointed his finger three times, not at the officer but beyond. "I wanna go to Tamarack," he yelled. "I wanna see my uncle."

McKay shoved his own arm out the window and ordered Liko to back up and move his car over onto a dirt parking area next to a dilapidated white barn. He was through playing this game. *The young punk thinks he has to answer to no one*, McKay must have thought. *Liko Kenney's sovereign nation, my ass.* The officer would have to teach Liko that there were rules to be obeyed and that *he* was the face of law and order in this small town.

With the Tamarack Tennis Camp now out of reach, Liko reluctantly followed the order. There was no place else he could go. He threw the Celica in reverse and backed into the dirt lot. Bruce McKay paused for a moment before pulling off the road. He noticed that a gray Chevy Silverado pickup truck had slowed down and stopped on the righthand shoulder of Route 116 next to the white barn. McKay waited seven seconds before pulling in after the Celica.

Sergeant David Wentworth was growing more concerned with each passing minute. He was still quite some distance from Route 116, but his driver, patrolman Phillip Blanchard, was making good time thanks to a shortcut he had suggested through Bickford Hill Road. *Geez, I haven't heard anything as far as updates from Corporal McKay,* Wentworth thought to himself. The Sugar Hill police sergeant thought this was unusual: McKay had always done things by the book and was generally very good about communicating with the police dispatcher. However, Wentworth also knew of a few times when Bruce McKay had either turned his radio down or off while conducting a police stop. *That must be why he's not answering.* Wentworth was sure this was no ordinary police stop. "Liko Kenney's name is one that I know of as being somebody the police have had dealings with," he would later tell investigators. "I haven't personally dealt with him, but I know that particularly Corporal McKay has had issues with him in the past." He had seen the dashcam video of the last McKay-Kenney encounter and it wasn't pretty. Wentworth could still hear the sound of Liko's wild screams ringing in his ears.

Liko Kenney was screaming once again. He had both hands raised in a defensive posture off the steering wheel. Bruce McKay's SUV was facing the Celica for the second time, but now he was ramming the vehicle with his own. McKay hit the gas pedal and the SUV jumped forward, striking the grill of the Toyota Celica with tremendous force. Both Liko and Caleb felt their heads snap back upon impact. McKay repeated the maneuver, this time with more power. The suv slammed into the front of Liko Kenney's car, pushing it back more than ten feet toward the steel teeth of a front-end loader and a rusted-out tractor that had been baking in the late afternoon sun. "No, no stop pushing my car," Liko screamed. McKay then jumped out of his police vehicle and strode swiftly over to Kenney's car. Liko put his left hand out once more. "What are you doing? What are you doing?" he asked anxiously.

Corporal McKay said nothing. Instead he held up a small container of pepper spray within a few inches of Liko's face and squirted it directly into the young man's eyes. Liko's head disappeared briefly in a cloud of yellowish toxic fog. The chemical also proved too potent for the officer, who quickly turned his back on Liko to escape the fumes. The oc gas (oleoresin capsicum) began working immediately, attacking Liko Kenney's eyes and lungs, blinding him but not delaying his reaction. As Caleb Macaulay was choking and covering his burning eyes in the passenger seat, Liko reached under his own seat, pulled out his gun, and fired several shots in the direction of the police officer.

If I wanted to shoot you,
you'd be God damned dead!
GREG FLOYD

Like Sergeant David Wentworth, the Grafton County dispatcher was also concerned that she had not been able to raise Bruce McKay on the radio. She shared her uneasiness with another unit heading in the direction of Easton Road. A few moments later time froze.

"Officer down, officer down . . . oh I don't . . . you need to come . . . I don't know where, you need to, you need to come," cried Gregory Paul Floyd over Bruce McKay's police radio. The teenager was shaking with fear. He jumped off the radio and returned two minutes later: "the police officer, I think he's dead and, and then they shoot at my, they shot at my dad and then he tried to run over the police officer. . . ."

Floyd's father, Greg Willis Floyd, later told investigators that he knew neither Bruce McKay nor the two young men in the Toyota; in fact, he had bumped into Liko Kenney and Caleb Macaulay just minutes before at Mac's Market (formerly Kelley's) in downtown Franconia. Greg and his eighteen-year-old son, Gregory, had traveled into town late in the afternoon to pick up a carton of milk, which they had forgotten during an earlier trip that day. As they entered the parking lot and found a handicap spot near the entrance of the store, a Toyota Celica pulled up to the empty space next to theirs. The two young men inside had drawn the elder Floyd's attention because their car bumped into the curb while they were trying to park. The Floyds entered the store and split up. Greg Floyd went to check the balance of their bank account, worried that recent work on his truck had left him overdrawn. He had gotten the brakes on his Chevy Silverado fixed earlier that day. At first, he thought the repairs would be around two hundred dollars. Floyd was thankful when the mechanic told him the bill would only top eighty bucks. During an earlier trip to Mac's Market, Floyd and his son had purchased a meat bundle that would cover the family for the next month or so. If the bank balance was managed frugally, there would be funds left over to pay the other bills that came along.

While dad was playing accountant, Gregory headed toward the dairy aisle. He picked up a carton of milk and also grabbed a jar of relish, a bottle of soda, and a copy of the local newspaper, the *Littleton Courier*, for his mother. He brought the items up to cashier Bonnie Russell, who was engaged in a conversation with a crew-cut young man in a green Agway shirt, later identified as Caleb Macaulay. Gregory had seen Caleb once before at the Agway when he and his father had gone there to buy topsoil to plant some trees. Caleb told the cashier that he and his friend were going to a party and expressed some frustration over the fact that he would have to pay five dollars to get in. Macaulay bought some boxes of Jell-O and cranberry juice while Liko waited outside smoking a cigarette. Caleb had paid no mind to Greg Floyd or his son. The father was a big man with a wide midsection, a balding crown, and thick eyeglasses. His son was several inches shorter but shared his father's girth. Gregory Floyd was an overweight teenager with curly blond hair who had been homeschooled since the fourth grade and was seen as even more of an outcast than Liko Kenney was. He was a teenager in limbo. Money was extremely tight in the Floyd household and Gregory had yet to take his high school equivalency exam or his driver's test because he could not afford the fees involved. His father was living on Social Security disability checks after undergoing sixteen back surgeries. Most of the money that came in, however, went back out to pay for medications for both him and his wife Michelle, who used a cane to walk and rarely left their house on Hummingbird Lane in Easton because of debilitating head, back, and leg injuries she had suffered during a car accident in 1996. Greg Willis Floyd was also a diabetic who took insulin three to five times a day to keep his blood sugar at a normal level. He had also survived a heart attack the previous November and was now on twenty-two other medications including the antidepressent Effexor, which carries a black box warning from the U.S. Food and Drug Administration on its label about the increased risk of suicidal thinking and behavior in young adults age eighteen to twenty-four during initial treatment. Greg Floyd was forty-nine and therefore apparently out of the danger zone. However, he could have been a candidate for Serotonin Syndrome, which the FDA describes as serious changes in how the brain, muscles, and digestive system work in response to high levels of serotonin in the body. Floyd was taking nearly two dozen medications a day. If he were using Effexor along with triptans to treat headaches, he would then be exposing himself to a number of side effects, including overactive reflexes and hallucinations. He appeared to be even and calm on this late afternoon.

After paying for their groceries, the Floyds drove across the street to Bob's Mobil station to buy gas for their chainsaw before getting back on Route 116 just a few minutes behind the Toyota Celica. Gregory was driving while his father sat comfortably in the passenger seat flipping through a real estate magazine. The younger Floyd had completed a driver's education course and was allowed to operate a motor vehicle without his license as long as he was accompanied by a legal guardian. Gregory had the radio playing and he was lost in his music as the landscape rolled by. Along their journey they passed the road up leading to the Robert Frost Museum. The renowned poet is the area's most famous former resident, having lived in Franconia from 1915 to 1920 and having enjoyed nineteen summers there with his family. They also drove by the quaint Franconia Inn, a white clapboard, three-story colonial-style retreat complete with riding stables. It was the New England scenery of postcards. Greg Willis Floyd was focused on his magazine and not the picturesque splendor surrounding him. He had been down this road thousands of times before. He had little reason to believe that this evening's ride home would be any different than those in the past.

Father and son continued down Route 116, approaching another inn, the Kinsman Lodge on the left. On the righthand side they noticed a Franconia police SUV facing another vehicle grill to grill. Greg Floyd ordered his son to slow down and pull off the road. "Did you see that guy give the cop the bird?" Gregory asked his father, misinterpreting Liko Kenney's hand gesture. The Floyds sat in their Chevy Silverado while Liko backed his Toyota into the dirt lot next to the weathered white barn. Greg Floyd watched and waited. The ex-Marine could sense that something was about to go down.

"Hey sir, can you just stay here for a minute as a witness?" Caleb Macaulay yelled over to Floyd. Suddenly, the police officer began pushing Kenney's car with his own vehicle. The Toyota was being shoved back toward two pieces of heavy equipment. Floyd heard screams coming from inside the Celica. He took his eyes off the Toyota for a couple of seconds to take in the entire scene. No other cars had driven by. It appeared that he and his son were the only witnesses to what was happening here. Then he heard the shots. They sounded like firecrackers, *rat-a-tat-tat* one after the other. Floyd turned back and saw Bruce McKay limping across the road. The officer's gun was now out of its holster and in his hand. The other hand was clutching his side like a marathoner fighting off a cramp. There was a stream of blood squirting from McKay's ribs that left behind a trail of red dots across the rippled pavement. Floyd grabbed his son and pulled him down below the dashboard of their truck and out of the line of fire.

Like Greg Floyd, Caleb Macaulay did not see Liko Kenney pull the trigger, but he heard the shots. He opened his eyes, still burning from the OC spray and saw the .45 Hi-Point semi-automatic pistol in his friend's hands. Caleb was shocked; he hadn't known

Liko had a gun in the car. Initially, he thought Liko had fired several warning shots in the air. Caleb did not see Bruce McKay get hit and assumed the officer had ducked for cover behind his SUV. Liko Kenney then backed up and sped out of the dirt parking lot and in the direction of Bruce McKay. Some will argue that he was blinded by pepper spray, while others insist he had lost his mind. Either way, Liko Kenney's next course of action may have overpowered his intent. He drove his Toyota Celica across Route 116 and plowed into a wounded Corporal McKay.

"He's bleeding Dad," Gregory Floyd told his father. "He doesn't look so good." *Oh shit, we're in the middle of this thing*, the elder Floyd thought to himself. He told his son to edge the truck up closer to where the officer was lying on a patch of grass on the opposite side of the road. At that moment, Liko Kenney backed up and struck McKay again from the back as the man struggled to get up. If the first attempt was an accident, the second certainly was not. Caleb Macaulay heard a thump and watched the hood of the car rise up and over the stricken cop. McKay's service weapon was sent flying by the force of the collision. "Go to the police cruiser and call for help," Floyd ordered his son. The ex-Marine then jumped out of his Chevy Silverado and walked quickly over to where McKay's gun lay on the grass. "At that point, I knew that I could take a chance and do something," Floyd would say later.

Liko Kenney turned his focus to his own gun. He was apparently trying to reload the weapon and did not see the stranger pick up Corporal McKay's Sig Sauer semi-automatic pistol. Greg Floyd checked the gun to see if it was chambered with a round. The hammer was still cocked back so Floyd made sure that he was careful with the inspection. He opened the chamber and found it loaded with a live round. He then looked back at the driver who appeared to be struggling with his pistol. Kenney was trying with both hands to unjam the gun. He would get one bullet in the chamber but the second bullet behind it would not let the slide shut.

Floyd approached the Toyota Celica silently. Liko did not notice the approach; instead he kept manipulating the firearm. Caleb saw the stranger walking toward them. The young man closed his eyes and ducked. He then heard the sound of shattering glass. At first, Caleb thought he had been shot. He felt a blast of air along the center of his back as the bullets flew by. He did not feel any pain, however. Maybe that was because his entire body was in shock. He pulled himself up in the passenger seat and saw the stranger standing outside the car door pointing a gun directly at him.

"Grab the gun and get the fuck outta the car," Greg Floyd yelled at him. Caleb looked over at his friend, who was not moving. Liko Kenney was covered with blood—his own. The .45 Hi-Point was clutched in his dead grip. "Grab the gun," Floyd commanded once more.

Caleb looked up at the stranger, who had a crazed look in his eyes. Macaulay was in hysterics himself, but he had to think clearly in order to save his own life. "Sir, if I give you this gun or if I touch this gun, you're gonna shoot me or try to shoot me."

"If I wanted to shoot you, you'd be God damned dead!" Floyd replied coldly.

🌿 For Susan Thompson, Easton Road in Franconia was home. It always had been home even during the thirty years she and her husband Chet had spent living and raising their children, Rebecca and Sarah, 163 miles away in Southborough, Massachusetts. Susan Thompson had grown up on this quiet country lane and had returned nearly every weekend over the next three decades to educate her two daughters about the wonders of the wilderness and to teach them how to ski at nearby Cannon Mountain. Skiing was in her blood and it was also the reason for her marriage to Chet Thompson. Chet, a flatlander from Massachusetts, was a longtime member of the Bumps and Bruises Ski Club and a director and officer for the Eastern Inter-club Ski League of Boston. The two met in March 1969 while Chet was volunteering as a race worker at the Eastern Championships at Cannon Mountain. Sue Thompson was teaching first and second grade in Sugar Hill at the time. The couple married a few months later and moved south because of Chet's job with a family-owned printing business. Sue was a grandmother now and she and her husband had spent the last nine years of their retirement running the Kinsman Lodge as a bed-and-breakfast. Like her neighbor Bill Kenney, who had been connected with the land around the Tamarack Tennis Camp for three generations, Sue Thompson's ties to the area went back even further. Her great-great-grandparents had purchased the Kinsman Lodge back in 1906 for eight hundred dollars, which included more than three hundred acres and the house next door where Sue later grew up. The inn itself had been built sometime in the 1860s and its name had changed often over the next hundred and forty years. Currently, it is called the Kinsman Lodge, named for Kinsman Mountain, which can be seen from the back door and tops 4,358 feet at its south peak. It's a cozy place where guests are often treated as members of the family.

In the early evening hours of May 11, 2007, Sue and her older sister Nancy Van Kleeck were in her office in a back room of the Kinsman Lodge, making a copy of a recipe, when they heard the wail of a police siren screaming past the house. Of course, they knew what a police siren sounded like, but hearing one on Easton Road was a very rare occurrence. Both women ran to the front door to see what the matter was. Susan looked outside and saw a gray car go by with a police vehicle directly behind it. The SUV was so close to the rear bumper of the Toyota Celica, Thompson first thought the police officer was attempting to pass the other driver and move on to some emergency down the road. Thompson wasn't getting a good-enough view at the door, so she walked into the inn's breakfast area where a big bay window overlooked Easton Road and the mountains beyond. Both vehicles had now come to a stop just a stone's throw from the lodge. Sue saw the gray car turn back into the dirt lot as the police SUV followed.

She was surprised to see the police cruiser pushing the car further into the lot. *Maybe the officer wants to get the driver off the road so that traffic can get by*, she thought. The theory vanished after she saw the SUV kick out a few inches of dirt from its back tires, pushing and pushing the Toyota until it was completely out of view. "I didn't see anything else for a short time, a very short time," she later told police. "Then I heard *pop pop*, I don't know how many times." The next thing Thompson saw was the officer clutching his chest as he attempted to cross the road. At that moment she ran into her kitchen and called 9-1-1.

❦ Thompson's daughter Rebecca Bell did witness Liko Kenney unload his .45 caliber Hi-Point on Corporal Bruce McKay. She had been standing in the kitchen when she first heard the police siren. She poked her head around the corner into the laundry room where a window gave her a clear view of Easton Road looking south. "I thought, oh, it's just another traffic stop. But then, it very quickly became evident that it was not a normal traffic stop," Bell informed investigators. She went outside on the front lawn of the Kinsman Lodge for a better look. When Kenney later pulled out his pistol and pulled the trigger, Bell figured it was a pellet gun or something smaller. She had never heard the sound of real gunshots before, but she expected it would be much louder. Like her mother, Rebecca Bell saw the officer turn and run across the street to her uncle's yard next door, but she didn't think he had been hit because he was moving so fast. "At that point, I came back inside because I realized that this was a more serious situation than we had initially thought. I also turned and looked and my daughter [one and a half years old] had let herself out and was on the back deck. So I swept her up and ran back inside." Bell handed her daughter over to her aunt Nancy as both her parents were dialing 9-1-1 from separate lines inside the lodge. In her frantic scramble to get help, Sue Thompson dialed 8-1-1 by mistake and got a recording for Dig Safe. She hung up and dialed again, this time making contact right away. "There have been shots fired," she told the dispatcher. "There's an officer injured."

Members of the Grafton County Sheriff's Department knew all too well what was happening. As Sue Thompson was alerting authorities to what was happening outside her inn, Gregory Paul Floyd was giving another dispatcher a blow-by-blow account of the drama as it continued to unfold around him. "The people that the officer was trying to stop all of a sudden just started shooting at him and then my dad had me stop and then he tried to help the officer," the teenager said between short breaths over Bruce McKay's radio. "Then they tried to shoot at him and run over the, my dad and the officer, their car is still over the officer and my dad is doing his best to keep the other one from trying to tackle him or something. . . . All I know is that these people just killed this officer and I, my dad had me come over and try to get help. I don't know what to do."

Sugar Hill Police Sergeant David Wentworth heard the radio dispatch and thought he was listening to a female's voice because the pitch was so high. He and Officer Phil Blanchard were making good time, but the winding road they were traveling on had slowed them down a bit. Wentworth had been on the force since 1991, splitting time between the Littleton, New Hampshire, police force and the department in Sugar Hill. Before that, he had been a K-9 handler in the security police for the U.S. Air Force stationed in South Korea. David Wentworth was as much a teacher as he was a cop. He was certified as an OC (oleoresin capsicum) and baton instructor and was now acting chief in Sugar Hill. His official title was executive officer in charge, and by all accounts he was the man running things in Sugar Hill since the police chief had taken a medical leave. Wentworth was also Phil Blanchard's supervisor and field training officer. A training criterion on which Blanchard was being evaluated was *stress driving*; that is, an officer's ability to get from point A to point B safely during a crisis situation. Wentworth ordered Blanchard to slow down a bit and stay in his lane of the narrow road while still reaching Easton Road in time to assist their comrade Bruce McKay. The latest dispatch told the officers that they were too late.

"Fuck, fuck!" Wentworth screamed. The veteran cop was confused. He had heard the words, "I think he's dead" during one of the radio calls but he didn't understand to whom the caller was referring. *Is it Bruce, or is it the bad guy?* he asked himself. *Who is it? What happened?* Wentworth's mind was filled with questions as he and Blanchard raced to the scene.

Alison Morris, a local real estate appraiser had just gotten off work and was out enjoying an early evening walk on Route 116 in the area of Wells Road. It had rained earlier in the day, but the storm clouds had given way to golden sunshine. "Franconia weather" is how the locals described the almost daily climate changes. Morris heard what she described as a "loud engine" off in the distance; as the vehicle making the sound drew closer, she recognized that it was Liko Kenney's Toyota Celica. Morris believed Kenney's car was moving too fast for this bumpy road. A few moments later, she saw Bruce McKay pass by in his police SUV. Morris watched as the cruiser turned around. As Morris continued her walk, she heard the police siren turn on and figured that Liko Kenney was not stopping for Corporal McKay.

Cindy Carpinetti, a pet shop owner in nearby Littleton, witnessed Bruce McKay's first attempt to pull Liko Kenney over. Carpinetti was in the area, debating whether to purchase a piece of land on the west side of Route 116. As she was leaving the parcel of land, traveling north in her red Ford Ranger, she spotted both vehicles stopped in a small horseshoe pull-off on the side of the road. As she passed the scene, she observed an older model car with "popup lights" speed off. Carpinetti told investigators that the officer then walked casually back to his vehicle and headed out after the car with his emergency lights activated.

Alison Morris's husband Richard had been up in the woods near the Kinsman Lodge, clearing brush from a mountain biking trail.

Richard Morris stopped what he was doing when he heard a series of pops. He turned to his friend, William Tucker Scheffer, and told him that it sounded like fireworks. Scheffer didn't know what it was or what direction the noise had come from. He reminded Morris that there was a shooting pit in the area. "If those were gunshots, it might be from that," Scheffer deduced. Both men shrugged and went back to work clearing the trail.

Rebecca Bell made sure that her daughter was safe and then ran back outside. "I'm gonna see if there's anything I can do to help," she told her parents. Bell had presumed that the gunman had left the scene and therefore the area was safe. As she entered the gravel parking lot next to the lodge, she noticed a large man standing beside the Toyota Celica with a gun in his hand. Realizing that the situation was ongoing and dangerous, Rebecca turned around and ran back inside the Kinsman Lodge. She waited there a few more minutes before she left the inn once again, walking this time in the opposite direction down Easton Road. Bell headed for Stanley and Lori Sherburn's house next door. Stanley was with the Franconia Fire Department and Rebecca figured that he could help keep oncoming traffic away from the volatile scene. Bell herself had stopped a car, informing the driver, "You need to turn around. You don't know what's going on. There's a person with a gun." Rebecca was also keeping a close eye out for her mother-in-law who was headed toward the Kinsman Lodge for a visit with her little granddaughter. *My God, now she's going to get caught up in this mess*, Bell thought.

Bill Kenney was trying to take a nap in his cabin on the grounds of the Tamarack Tennis Camp when he was startled by the sound of a police siren. It had already been an exhausting day for the "gentleman farmer." The previous evening, he had picked up his mother-in-law at JFK airport in New York and had driven 344 miles back to Franconia, arriving at approximately 1 A.M. on May 11. Kenney got a couple of hours' sleep before putting in a full day with his wife Larisa and her mother. By 5 P.M. Bill was exhausted, so he climbed into bed with his wife and had even turned off his computer to block out any ambient noise. The moment he closed his eyes, he heard the distant wail of a siren followed shortly thereafter by the sound of firecrackers. He heard a similar noise a few minutes later. What he could not hear were his nephew's cries for help. Kenney got up, put his boots back on, and went outside to investigate. As he was leaving his cabin, he saw Holly Miller, the wife of his former brother-in-law Woody Miller, walking past him on the trail. She appeared completely dazed. "Liko's been killed," she told him.

Bill's brother Michael arrived at the scene fifteen minutes later; he had spent the day paving a tennis court in Vermont. "Cops were flying about everywhere," he says. "Somehow, I knew right away it was Liko. When I heard that McKay was involved also, I figured he [McKay] had done something to escalate it."

Jack Kenney arrived in the wilds of Franconia, New Hampshire, in 1946, nearly four decades before the birth of his grandson Liko. Jack Kenney was a flatlander from Reading, Massachusetts, where there were plenty of opportunities for servicemen returning from the war. The town was just ten miles north of Boston and was home to several businesses including Addison-Wesley, a publishing company that specialized in technical and scientific books. There is no doubt Jack Kenney could have made a prosperous living but the young man yearned for adventure. He and Bob Allard, a friend from his navy days, were looking to open a ski lodge, although Franconia was not their first choice. Initially, they had traveled to North Conway, which was home to several bustling ski mountains, including Cranmore and nearby Attitash and Wildcat. Winter sports enthusiasts had been introduced to North Conway during the 1930s when "snow trains" began carrying visitors north from Boston to the area that would eventually become known as "the birthplace of American skiing." Jack Kenney and his partner found the land in North Conway a bit too expensive and were told they might find something cheaper on the other side of the White Mountains. The pair made their way through Crawford Notch and located an ideal spot in the small village of Easton, just over the Franconia town line and within easy driving distance of Cannon Mountain. Franconia was much smaller than North Conway, but had also enjoyed a thriving tourist trade thanks to the popularity of The Old Man of the Mountain.

One of the area's first hotels was the Lafayette House, also known as Gibb's Hotel and built in 1835 on the southeast base of Cannon Mountain. The Lafayette House was large enough to accommodate fifty guests and served the area for nearly two decades before a larger, grander hotel, the Profile House, was constructed nearby. In 1853, the Lafayette House was moved across the Notch road to the back of the Profile House where it was used as a workroom and laundry before it was later renovated into a dormitory for waitresses. The Old Lafayette House, as it was now called was modernized again in 1897 with an added third story and was converted into a new cottage to house both female and male employees. While the Lafayette could only house about four dozen guests, the Profile House had been built to accommodate up to six hundred people comfortably. It boasted the largest dining room in New England and, with its stately guest rooms, billiard hall, bowling alley, and music room, the luxurious setting and tranquil surroundings of the Profile House drew wealthy patrons from the United States and Europe. Among the guests were President Ulysses S. Grant, circus promoter P. T. Barnum (who once dressed hotel workers as animals and performed a circus for guests), William H. and Cornelius Vanderbilt, and several other members of high-society arbiter Ward McAllister's Four Hundred (his list of the four hundred most prominent New Yorkers). The author of one local guidebook wrote that the Profile House offered interesting excursions for "men of action," while "quieter souls" could relax on comfortable verandas surrounded by the "rich beauty of forests and cliff." Tourism quickly became a major source of revenue for the White Mountains, generating more than a million dollars annually by 1874. The region survived relatively unscathed through the economic turbulence that plagued much of the nation in the 1890s, following strikes at the Homestead Steel Mills in Pennsylvania and Chicago's Pullman Company. The unemployment rate soared as high as 20 percent, but the White Mountains saw its seasonal revenues fall only once: around 1893, when millions of

Americans spent their summer vacations visiting the World's Fair in Chicago.

In 1905, the Profile House was completely torn down and replaced by a new and even more spectacular hotel that offered tennis, croquet, and badminton. Guests were the only people allowed to enjoy nearby Profile Lake, which was kept stocked with trout. The second Profile House operated for only sixteen years before it burned to the ground in 1922. Innkeeper Karl Abbott wrote down what he witnessed that fateful night: "The entire entrance to the Notch was a blazing inferno against which the puny efforts of man were inconsequential. By the time I arrived our beautiful little mountain community was an area of smoldering ashes. A state of chaos prevailed in the ruined Notch." The exact cause of the fire was never determined.

Gilded hotels added to the Franconia area's charm, but did not define it. This was still nature's domain. The area's second most popular attraction—after the Old Man of the Mountain— was a breathtaking natural gorge known as the Flume. The gorge, located on the western side of Mount Flume, was formed millions of years ago when coffee-colored molten lava pushed through the granite, forming dikes when it cooled. The biggest dike was worn down over centuries, eventually creating the gorge we see today. According to legend, it was discovered in June 1808 by a ninety-three-year-old pioneer named Jess Guernsey (Aunt Jess, as she was called by her family and friends), who was searching for a new place to fish. Guernsey had often heard the distant roar of running water from her family's log home at the base of Mount Pemigewasset, but she had never actually seen it before. With a fishing pole in one hand, Guernsey used the other to clear branches as she navigated her way through the thicket toward the sound of the rushing water that grew louder as she drew closer. The old woman stood agape at the sight of the canyon, eight hundred feet long, and the cascading waterfalls and granite walls that were ninety feet high but seemed to rise up to the heavens. Aunt Jess had forgotten all about fishing; instead, she rushed home and told her husband David what she had just seen. Guernsey's trek was later romanticized by the poet Harry Hibbard:

> And farther down from Guernsey's lone abode,
> By a rude footpath climb the mountainside,
> Leaving below the travelers' winding road,
> To where the cleft hill yawns abrupt and wide,
> As tho some earthquake did its mass divide
> In olden time; there view the Rocky Flume,
> Tremendous chasm! Rising side by side,
> The rocks abrupt wall in the long, high room,
> Echoing the wild stream's roar, and dark with vapory gloom.
> (from the poem "Franconia Mountain Notch," 1839)

"Dark" and "gloomy" are words used by Bill Kenney to describe his mother Peg, whom Jack had met during a ski trip to Lake Tahoe, California, while on leave from the USS *Belleau Wood* in late autumn 1944. Peg Taylor also came from a military background; her father was a graduate of the U.S. Military Academy at West Point and had taught there before taking his wife and three children, Peg being the youngest, out to the West Coast when she was a child. Bill Kenney paints a vivid picture of his mother as a young woman. "She was rebellious and a real tomboy," he explains. "She'd do anything the boys did, but she'd do it better and faster than the boys did." The matriarch of the Kenney clan later studied sociology at the University of California at Berkeley. Bill Kenney says these were not formative years: "There were other things playing in her soul, darkness in her soul from the past. Her father died when she was twelve and I think some darkness came from that. She was carrying some demons with her right through her life." Athleticism, rebellion, and darkness were traits she passed down to her children and her grandchildren.

Darkness could also be found in Jack Kenney's soul. He had never gotten over his mother's suicide, which had followed his father's death just after Jack had graduated from college. He was also most likely stricken by what psychiatrists call "survivor's guilt." He may have been struggling with it on the day he met his future wife. It must have been an odd feeling for the young naval officer as he strapped on his skis and gazed out at the crystallized white powder blanketing the sun-splashed slopes, knowing that he was not supposed to be there. Just weeks earlier, he could only watch as nearly a hundred of his shipmates were burned alive. Until that point, the men of the USS *Belleau Wood* had been fortunate; some might even say lucky. The aircraft carrier had taken part in thirteen raids in the Pacific theater, including the epic battles for Tarawa and Wake Island. Later, in the Battle of the Philippine Sea, *Belleau Wood*'s fighter planes sank the mighty Japanese carrier *Hiyo* as the imperial navy was making its retreat. The Japanese carriers *Zuikaku*, *Junyo*, and *Chitose* were also heavily damaged. More than four hundred Japanese fighter planes were destroyed during the onslaught, while 90 percent of American pilots made it back to their ships alive. The one-sided U.S. military victory became known as the Great Marianas Turkey Shoot. The Japanese would have their revenge four months later on October 30, 1944, when a kamikaze pilot caught a shell from a nearby American ship and, knowing he was going to crash, directed his doomed plane toward the rear flight deck of the *Belleau Wood*, igniting a rash of fires and ammunition explosions that resulted in the deaths of ninety-two of Jack Kenney's fellow crewmen. The recovery was as traumatic as the fiery blasts had been. Jack and his shipmates spent the evening trying to hose down fires that continued to flare up on the charred carrier while the bodies of friends were being stacked like cords of wood around them.

The battered USS *Belleau Wood* eventually sailed into San Francisco's Hunter's Point naval base for extensive repairs; the survivors were granted much-needed rest and relaxation. For Jack, relaxation meant a trip to the nearest ski mountain. The native New Englander had never skied before, but he was somehow fascinated by the romance of opening a ski lodge back home should he survive the war. He couldn't control his mortality any more than any other man, woman, or child could, but he *could* learn how to ski. He found the perfect teacher at the Sugar Bowl ski resort in Lake Tahoe. Peg Taylor had just graduated from Berkeley and had the reputation of being the fastest member of the U.S. women's ski team. The ski lesson lasted just one day, but Peg's energy and unbridled enthusiasm stayed with Jack when his air group was reassigned to the USS *Monterey*, an Independence Class light-aircraft carrier whose crewmembers included a young assistant navigator named Gerald R. Ford (who thirty years later would become the thirty-eighth president of the United States). While serving on the USS *Monterey*, Jack Kenney, now a full lieutenant, had been assigned to naval intelligence, briefing bomber squadrons on the logistics and climate conditions of each mission. Jack and Peg wrote each other repeatedly over the next year as the war finally wound down. Following Japan's surrender to Allied forces in August 1945, Jack was sent home to begin a new phase of his life.

He told Peg about his plans to settle in New Hampshire, a region he had fallen in love with during his years as a student at Dartmouth College in Hanover, where he studied economics and graduated second in his class. He was also a force on the athletic fields: the 1934 edition of *Aegis*, the Dartmouth College yearbook, records that Jack won high praise from the coaching staff of the football team for his powerful blocking that helped lead them to a 41 to 0 trouncing of Norwich Academy. Jack had later gone on to receive his master's degree in education at the University of New Hampshire in Durham. After college, he spent two years in the northern mill town of Berlin, where he taught history and tennis at the high school before enlisting in the navy after the attack on Pearl Harbor. The war was over now and somehow he had survived. The horrors he had witnessed remained with him like a constant companion, but also gave him the fortitude to lead his life *his way*, unconventional and eclectic.

Jack Kenney and Bob Allard paid $10,000 for 450 acres of Franconia farmland that included a house and a barn. His dream of opening a ski lodge was close to becoming reality now. Jack even had a name for it, Tamarack Lodge, but he needed a staff to run the place. He convinced Peg and a friend to move east to help with the cooking and cleaning. A year after getting settled in Franconia, Jack Kenney traded in his partner for a wife. He bought out Bob Allard after the first season. There were no hard feelings: in fact, Bob Allard got engaged to Peg's friend Mimi. Both couples drove cross-country to get married, but only Jack and Peg would return to Tamarack Lodge, named for the tamarack trees that stood tall by the roadside. The tamarack tree is described as the most cold-hardy of any native tree in North America, with the strongest wood of all the conifers. Strong and cold-hardy could describe Jack and Peg Kenney as well. The early years of the Tamarack Lodge were a mighty struggle for the young couple. Much like Jess Guernsey and the other pioneers who had fought to carve out a life in the New Hampshire wilderness, Jack and Peg Kenney found themselves living day to day, wondering whether they would have enough to keep the lodge running and to feed their growing brood. "It was real nip and tuck," Bill Kenney remembers. "The lodge would get booked up for Christmas and New Year's, and then all of a sudden you'd get a thaw—cancellations. Nobody comes." Jack tried to keep the lodge from going under by going away in search of work. During those first summers he traveled down to places like Newport, Rhode Island, and North Carolina—anywhere he could pick up some extra money teaching tennis to the rich. Still, the bills piled up. During this time, Jack also became skilled at the art of diversion. He wrote about the financial challenges of running a small business in a humorous article for *Hospitality* magazine:

A shopping trip to town is an adventure. You walk across Main Street dodging creditors like a halfback dodging tacklers. A quick dash across the road to avoid the insurance man, a dart down the alley to avoid the oil man. The inevitable happens and you bump headlong into one of them and he opens up with, "Now how about that . . ." But you interrupt him with the rosy story that Old Farmer's Almanac predicts a big winter, and so very shortly he'll have his due.

Peg Kenney's dark mood became more evident when the times got tough. Her brooding could only be broken by the adrenalin rush she felt barreling down a mountain. She skied hard and fast, winning national races and coming just shy of landing a spot on the U.S. Olympic ski team for the 1948 winter games in St. Moritz, Switzerland. Her hard-charging style on the slopes can be seen today in her grandson, Bode Miller, who described Peg Kenney in his autobiography, *Bode: Go Fast, Be Good, Have Fun*: "She was reckless, especially for a young woman then. She drove like a bank robber, drank whiskey from the bottle, loved to gamble, and was a kick-ass competitor" (9).

Peg Kenney loved to gamble, but putting her chips down on the unpredictability of winter weather, even in New Hampshire, was a bet she could not win. Jack and Peg had to come up with a plan that would increase the chances of steady revenue. They transformed the lodge once more in 1962, this time into a tennis camp for kids, the first of its kind in New England. Jack had built a strong reputation as a tennis instructor on the grass courts of Newport. Teaching tennis was second nature to Jack: he began coaching the sport during his days as a teacher at Berlin High School, and he was a natural mentor for the young students of the game. He developed the Tamarack learning method, founded on simple repetition, innovative games, and promoting confidence in campers so that one day they could learn to be their own teacher. He had even designed a machine, which he called "Charlie," to help players practice. Basically, it was a vacuum cleaner with a reverse suction. The steady air kept the tennis ball floating in perpetual motion. Players could work alone on their swings, much as young baseball players do with T-ball. Years later, Jack also developed methods to teach disabled children at the Crotched Mountain Rehabilitation Center in Greenfield, New Hampshire. Using an inclined tube filled with tennis balls, Jack put together a serving machine that would release balls slowly, allowing any child in a wheelchair or lacking motor skills development sufficient time to hit the ball.

The tennis camp's reputation spread and soon youngsters began turning up with their tennis racket, a bag of clothes, and an appreciation for the rustic, no-frills atmosphere that Jack and Peg Kenney worked so hard to cultivate. They only saw ten campers the first season, but the number grew to one hundred just five years later. Jack and Peg Kenney also worked hard to instill this back-to-basics attitude in their own children: Jo, Bill, Davey, Bubba, and Mike. Nonetheless, the children developed a love-hate relationship with Tamarack. Jack Kenney often said, "My children grew up in a business, not a family." Most times, the campers were treated better than the kids were. When camp was in session, the Kenney children were kicked out of their bedrooms and forced to sleep elsewhere on the grounds. Life at Tamarack could be tough, but the surroundings were paradise. Each day was an adventure for the children, who could explore babbling brooks, trickling streams, and winding dirt paths that seemed to stretch for miles. The children loved nature and fought those who dared to defile it. In fact, the Kenney kids became eco-terrorists of sorts when developers encroached on the land surrounding their beloved Tamarack Tennis Camp. "If someone was planning to build a condo complex or hotel nearby, the Kenneys would try to sabotage the project," says family friend and former tennis instructor Tom Gross. "They'd fill the tractor engines and gas tanks with sand so they wouldn't be able to move." The Kenneys considered the outside world a serious threat to their way of life. "The kids wanted to live on the land, smoke their pot, and be left alone," Gross says. Jack Kenney was arrested for growing marijuana on the Tamarack grounds in 1969 when he was fifty-three years old. Jack protested his innocence immediately saying he had no idea where the plants had come from. He was quickly exonerated when four students from nearby Franconia College admitted the pot plants were theirs.

❦ Franconia College served as a beacon of light for a generation of hippies hoping to stay one step ahead of the draft board and out of the jungles of Vietnam. It first opened in 1963 as a two-year liberal arts college on the site of the old Forest Hills Hotel on Agassiz Road. Franconia College began granting four-year degrees two years later, in 1965. The students were as unconventional as the coursework. Many chose to live in tents and tepees in the woods (where they could keep a watchful eye on their marijuana harvest). In school, students learned to tap trees in a course called Sugar Maple Wood Lot Management. The maple syrup would then be sold to raise money for the college. Professors also taught auto repair and the physics department had even formed a UFO sighting group.

Spaceship spotting, however, was not the only extracurricular activity to draw notice from outsiders. Among the school's critics was William Loeb, conservative publisher of the Manchester *Union Leader*. The *Union Leader* was New Hampshire's most prominent newspaper and the publisher's editorials were often splashed across the front page. William Loeb was right-wing to the core. His pro-establishment attitude mirrored that of New Hampshire's blue-collar workers, who lived by their guns and by the United States Constitution. The publisher's attitude was Live Free or Die—provided you don't grow your hair long or hold subversive thoughts. For William Loeb, there were no gray areas. "Things are either right or they are wrong," he was known to say. His ideological hero was the red-baiting senator Joe McCarthy. Loeb was so enamored of McCarthy's communist-hunting campaign that he called Republican president Dwight D. Eisenhower "a stinking hypocrite" for not supporting the Wisconsin lawmaker after the Senate voted overwhelmingly to condemn him in 1954. Loeb saved most of his vitriolic volleys for Democrats though. He referred to FDR's successor as Harry "General Incompetence" Truman and once called John F. Kennedy "the No. 1 liar in America."

William Loeb was viewed by some as nothing more than a rich, aging crackpot, but others knew better. Despite the fact that his newspaper had a small circulation (65,298 subscribers), Loeb wielded formidable power in the state that held the nation's first presidential primary. The publisher flexed his political muscles when he helped derail Edmund Muskie's presidential bid in 1972. Muskie was a two-time governor of and then U.S. senator from Maine, whom many considered the best hope to beat President Richard Nixon. Those hopes crashed and burned on a snowy day just two weeks before the New Hampshire primary thanks to a pair of derisive editorials written by William Loeb. In one editorial, Loeb published a letter from a Florida man accusing Muskie of laughing at an ethnic slur against French-Canadians—who just happened to make up a large voting bloc in New Hampshire. The letter was later proved to be a hoax, planted by President Nixon's "dirty tricks" squad. The second editorial suggested that Muskie's wife, Jane, had a drinking problem and spoke like a sailor while stumping for her husband on the campaign trail. Muskie responded with a tearful defense of his wife outside the offices of the Manchester *Union Leader*. With his voice cracking, Muskie called William Loeb "a gutless coward" for attacking his wife. Reporters covering the news conference wrote that the six-foot-four statesman was reduced to tears by Loeb's barbs. Muskie's campaign staffers claimed the wetness on the candidate's cheeks was caused by falling snow, not tears. The spin control was not effective for the longtime front-runner. Muskie managed to eke out a small victory over South Dakota senator George McGovern in New Hampshire, but the dark-horse candidate went on to defeat Muskie for the Democratic nomination.

When William Loeb wasn't railing against left-leaning politicians, he was focused on the growing scourge of marijuana-smoking hippies settling in his beloved Granite State. Four years before the Muskie editorials, Loeb printed an article by Arthur C. Egan, "Bare Debauchery at Franconia College: Sex, Liquor, Drugs Rampant on Campus." The attention and weight Loeb had given the article is evident in its placement on the *Union Leader*'s front page — *above* the masthead. Such a headline would raise some eyebrows even on a slow news day, but it is truly astounding to see that Egan's so-called exposé was given editorial priority over the day's real lead story: the assassination of the Reverend Dr. Martin Luther King, Jr. "A wonderful dream has turned into a nightmare," he wrote. "College policy allows virtually unlimited license to students and faculty alike in the pursuit of academic studies and personal pleasures. Drugs, alcohol and sex are among the main ingredients in campus life." Many students criticized the article, calling it an "exaggerated view" of Franconia College. Even if it weren't an exaggerated view, the year was 1968 — a time of political unrest and sexual freedom on college campuses across the nation. Why Loeb and Egan had chosen to single out Franconia College may come down to simple revenge. After all, the long-haired, unwashed students from Franconia College made up the majority of protesters who had marched repeatedly in front of the *Union Leader* to voice their anger over the war in Vietnam. William Loeb wanted them out of his sight and out of his state.

The plan worked even better than the publisher had probably hoped. The article sparked a panic among the school's board of trustees, who took swift action and fired the college president. Soon after, twenty faculty members also resigned and a third of the student population either quit school or went to study elsewhere. It did not take long before Franconia College declared bankruptcy. The school rebounded briefly in 1970 when twenty-three-year-old Harvard doctoral candidate Leon Botstein took over the reins, becoming the youngest college president in America. Botstein recruited professors willing to work for low money and no tenure while securing $800,000 in federal grants to help the school dig out from a huge financial hole. The Doogie Howser of college presidents also helped take some of the tarnish off the school's battered reputation. Leon Botstein was profiled by *Time* magazine, and the college itself was later the subject of a feature story on the *ABC Evening News*. The publicity wasn't enough, however, to keep the school operating in the long run. Franconia College closed its doors for good in 1978, months after conferring an honorary degree on world heavyweight boxing champion Muhammad Ali.

Most Franconians had shunned the freethinking, free-loving ways of the local college population, but the Kenney clan had embraced it. Outsiders were welcome at Tamarack as long as they shared the Kenney family's left-wing worldview and frontier spirit. Jo Kenney's boyfriend, Woody Miller, was one of those like-minded dreamers. Woody was an instructor at the tennis camp and a medical student at the University of Vermont. Woody's real name was John, which his father had insisted on calling him. His father had also insisted that his son study to become a doctor, as he and Woody's two older brothers had done. Just as skiing and tennis were traditions in the Kenney household, medicine was a tradition for the Millers. In fact, Woody's grandfather had been president of the American Medical Association and his father was a renowned heart surgeon. But Woody Miller had other plans. He knew that if he just up and quit school, his father would hound him for a lifetime. Instead, Woody, determined to flunk out, burned all his notes and books just two weeks before final exams. His plan didn't work; he passed his exams. Beaten but unbowed, Woody persisted; eventually he flunked pediatrics and was not asked back to UVM.

Woody took the rejection as gleefully as if he had just won the lottery. He moved to Easton, New Hampshire, married Jo Kenney and built a log cabin of his own next to a stream on the Kenney family land nearly a mile off the main road. They built their log cabin using the same methods of the pioneers. They carried the materials up the steep hill themselves and then pieced the wood together, mostly without the use of electric tools. Woody and Jo were hippies and also political activists. Woody founded the Turtle Party (The United Resolution to Love Earth) in 1982. The manifesto was simple: much like a turtle, party members strived for patience and hard work as well as inclusion and thoughtfulness. Woody summed up the idea of love this way, "a feeling of strong personal attachment induced by that which delights or commands admiration." The couple homeschooled their children, Kyla, Bode, Chelone, and Wren (short for Genesis Wren Bungo Windrushing Turtleheart) and lived the Kenney way, without electricity or phones. A simple trip to the bathroom meant leaving the cabin, crossing the stream, and walking up a hill to an outhouse. Woody and Jo Kenney split up in 1985 (when Bode was four). It happened after a brief experiment with communal living. Woody and Jo had placed an ad in the *Mother Earth News* seeking likeminded couples to come to Franconia where they could grow food and raise children together. But Woody took the idea of communal living a step too far: he had an affair with one of the women who had answered their ad and Jo Kenney called it quits. Woody moved away to Nashville for a while before eventually returning to Tamarack and forging a truce with Jo for the sake of the kids. Jo moved out of the log cabin they had built together and Woody moved back in—with a new wife he had met while living down south. They raised the kids there while their mother lived nearby.

Davey and Michele Kenney had set up their home down the hill and across Easton Road. Like the rest of the clan, their cabin was spartan. But unlike his brothers and sister, Davey was not cut out for the harsh winter climate of northern New England. He dreamed of a tropical paradise and found it in his early twenties, thousands of miles away in Hawaii. Davey would make it back to Tamarack every summer to get the best of both worlds, and one year he brought with him a wife. Michele Kenney had moved to Hawaii because she too had grown averse to the cold winters of her native state. "Her father was a cook on a tanker in the Great Lakes," brother-in-law Bill Kenney explains. "They lived way up in northern Wisconsin and she [Michele] had a bad experience when she was young. They had seven kids in the family and they were out ice skating one winter day and a family friend was supposed to pick them up. He never did and Michele was left waiting on a road and the temperatures dropped to about 20 below zero and they almost perished. She really does not like winter."

In Hawaii, the couple operated a small coffee farm that was anything but profitable. They drove beat-up cars and rarely had any money—not that money was all that important to them. They found their wealth in the beauty of the place. They built their oasis on twenty acres surrounded by hundred-year-old Japanese pine trees nearly a mile up a mountain in a cloud forest. The couple even had to build their own road. It was like Tamarack Hawaiian style. Davey and Michele lived off the grid with no electricity. Michele likened it to living in the middle of the jungle. Coffee was not the only crop growing on the Kenney farm. Davey also found satisfaction and peace in his pot plants. "Davey smoked marijuana basically every day of his life," Bill Kenney explains. "He had a really bad temper in his early teens, and I was fearful for him." Bill described his brother as a skinny kid who never backed down from a fight. "He was a real wise guy with a temper, and then he started smoking pot and it just turned him right around. I consider that a classic example of medicinal marijuana."

Bill says that Davey, the youngest of Jack and Peg Kenney's children, was an unwanted child and that his doubt and lack of confidence was passed down to his first child, a boy that he and Michele named Liko Peter Kenney. The child was different from the very beginning. He was one of the few members of the clan born at a hospital and not on the grounds of Tamarack. Jo Miller had served as midwife for the delivery. "There were terrible complications," she recalls. "Michele's bladder descended when she went into labor and we had to rush her to Littleton Regional Hospital." Michele Kenney spent nineteen painful hours in labor before delivering Liko to the world. "He was blocked and couldn't come out," Jo explains. "I think it set into his personality. Liko always felt as if there was something in his way."

"Michele wanted to have kids and Davey didn't," Bill Kenney claims. "This eventually had an effect on Liko." As a boy, Liko rebelled against his rebellious family by choosing not to ski, which was the lifeblood of the Kenney clan. Even Davey, who didn't like winter, loved to hit the slopes. Uncle Mike Kenney says Liko was also the only Kenney cousin to never take part in the soccer clinics at the Tamarack camp. Liko did share in his family's passion for political activism, though. Jack McEnany, coauthor of *Bode: Go Fast, Be Good, Have Fun*, wrote about his earliest memory of Liko (then seven years old) on his blog: "We were at a Seabrook anti-nuke demonstration and he cajoled the couple on the blanket next to us to carve up their watermelon and pass it around. Liko never lost that naïve sweetness; he was a loyal friend, a good-hearted soul, and a wild kid. But in a good way, mostly" (www.Lostnation .tv, May 2007).

Even so, Liko and his younger sister Mahina were still seen as outsiders in a family of outsiders. Some family members, including Bill Kenney, referred to the children as "the Polynesians." Liko and Mahina both had long hair down to their waist and both were known to frolic around the grounds of the Tamarack Tennis Camp without any clothes. They seemed more suited to Rudyard Kipling's *The Jungle Book* than to the wooded hills of Franconia Notch. But where Mahina would be described as "sweet and full of light," young Liko had been cursed with the same darkness that had plagued his grandparents, Jack and Peg Kenney. "I wouldn't call Liko disturbed," Bill Kenney says. "But he was wild and crazy. Let's call it wild and crazy." The boy also had a mean streak and a penchant for violence. Jo Miller remembers one incident when

Liko was just a toddler: "I had to pin his arms down because he kept reaching for a kitchen knife to stab a friend of Davey's who had picked up his toy." Jo Miller had seen the same fire in her own son Chelone, who was Liko's kindred spirit growing up: "They terrorized Tamarack. They wrecked everything." It appeared that no one could escape the boys' wrath. The troublesome pair picked on campers who were smaller than they were and frequently trashed bikes that didn't belong to them. The boys even liberated their grandmother Peggy's prized brass BBQ skewers and tried to melt them. Eventually the boys were banished from Tamarack altogether. "They were ordered not to show their faces around the camp during the summer," Jo Kenney says. "They were just too unpredictable."

Liko's temper grew more volatile as he got older. Some of his friends even expressed reservations about being alone with him. One longtime pal, Matthew Chernicki, described Liko Kenney as a "sociopath." Chernicki later told investigators about a dark joke shared among the young man's friends: "On a hike with Liko, you never knew if you were going to come back." Liko's friends were not the only people nervous around him; his family was, as well. Jo Kenney claims that he had a bad relationship with his younger sister Mahina. "When he wasn't terrorizing Tamarack, he was terrorizing his home," Kenney claims. "When he couldn't pick on the campers at Tamarack, he turned his sights on his little sister." According to Jo Kenney, when Mahina left for Antioch College in Ohio, she vowed never to come back to Franconia so long as her brother was there.

For Liko Kenney, however, there would be no college. Diagnosed with dyslexia in his teens, Liko struggled mightily in the classroom. The condition no doubt frustrated the young man, who by all accounts was extremely bright and well spoken. Davey and Michele brought in specialists to work with their son but there would be no breakthrough and Liko dropped out of Profile High School. He had no job and no real prospects but Liko Kenney did have many friends to lean on in these turbulent years during his late teens and early adulthood. One of those friends was Seery Hayward, who also struggled with dyslexia. If Chelone Kenney was Liko's kindred spirit as a young boy, Seery Hayward certainly filled that role as a young adult. They hung around the North Country together, smoking pot and living from party to party. Privately they must have discussed the limited options facing them in the future. The remoteness of Franconia made it a difficult place to live, even if one had a job. For Liko Kenney, it was a dead-end street surrounded by mountains. Seery could see the anger building in his friend. He had told his father Rob Hayward several times that he was worried about Liko's attitude. "He's gonna get in trouble or hurt," he said. "Or he's gonna hurt someone else."

Jo Kenney believes her nephew's rage was fueled by his intelligence. "He was a smart kid and he knew it," she says. "But the dyslexia kept him in a prison of sorts and when other people talked down to him he had a very hard time dealing with it." When his father faced trouble for building a small cabin for his son on the Tamarack grounds without a permit, Liko forced a showdown with Franconia selectmen at a town meeting. "He walked in with his Bowie knife strapped to his leg and a copy of the United States Constitution in his hands," Davey remembers. "He then proceeded to lecture the town fathers about the Constitution and the Bill of Rights. Some members got a real kick out of it, while others didn't know what to make of him."

When Liko wasn't stewing in his anger, he was contemplating his own mortality. This fixation may have been heightened by the deaths of two of his close friends, who had been killed within months of each other. The first was his buddy Tommy Giaccobe, who drowned during a boating accident in Crested Butte, Colorado, in June 2005. The second was an even bigger blow: Seery Hayward was driving home in the early hours of September 24, 2005, when he fell asleep at the wheel and overturned his pickup truck. Seery had not been wearing a seatbelt and was ejected from the vehicle. This loss had a profound effect on Liko Kenney, who could not let his dear friend go. On May 10, 2007, just one day before the deadly confrontation with Bruce McKay and Greg Floyd, Liko visited Seery's father with a few friends, including Caleb Macaulay. The young men spent a few minutes chatting with Rob Hayward before Liko arrived, emerging from some nearby woods covered with ticks. "What the hell were you doing in there?" Hayward asked, as he helped pick a small army of ticks off Liko's skin and clothing. "I had to talk to Seery," Liko said matter-of-factly. The friends had a secret gathering spot in the thick brush near Seery's house where they used to drink beer and smoke pot. "What'dya mean you had to talk to Seery?" Rob Hayward asked. "You don't undertant. I had to talk to Seery," Liko reiterated, more forcefully this time. Hayward took Liko by the arm and pulled him gently away from his buddies. "Why did you have to talk to my son?" Hayward whispered.

"Something's gonna happen tomorrow," Liko told him.

"What're you talking about?"

"Something's gonna happen tomorrow. I don't know what, but Seery told me that I have to protect Caleb," Liko explained as he nodded to his friend standing in the distance. Rob Hayward immediately thought back to a previous conversation with Liko, when the young man told him that local police were gunning for him. "They're gonna kill me someday," Liko predicted. "They'll never take me alive." This wasn't a James Cagney–style boast. Liko Kenney had convinced himself that if Bruce McKay came after him again, he would not be given a chance to surrender peacefully: "He'll kill me before that happens."

Caleb Macaulay could not move. Caleb Macaulay would not move. He sat crouched in the passenger seat of Liko Kenney's Toyota Celica staring up at the barrel of a .45 caliber Sig Sauer semi-automatic pistol. The bottles of vodka and cranberry juice remained unopened in a bag in the back seat. Within just a few short violent minutes the young man's world had been turned upside down. Since morning, he had been looking forward to this part of the day, a time to relax and have a few drinks with his close friend. Now his friend was dead in the seat next to him, a lifeless mass covered in blood. Caleb couldn't tell whether Liko had been shot in the chest or the face. "He had blood splattered all over the car, all over him," Macaulay recalled later. Caleb was surprised that he too wasn't covered in blood. He was understandably shaken by the sight of his friend. He had seen a few dead people before, but that had been while he was attending a funeral or a wake, and the dead were always made to look quite peaceful in their open caskets. There was nothing peaceful about the death of Liko Kenney. Caleb figured that he would be the next one to die if he followed the stranger's orders to grab Liko's gun. Greg Floyd shouted his demand once more, but Caleb refused to comply. Floyd then reached into the passenger-side window and elbowed Macaulay in the throat before extending his arm into Liko's lap and prying the .45 caliber Hi-Point out of his fingers. The ex-Marine then ordered Caleb out of the vehicle. "Get outta the car and get on your knees," Floyd ordered. "And if you move, I'm gonna blow your face off." Macaulay fumbled with his seat belt and opened the car door with his hands raised.

He sat Indian style on the ground and placed his hands on top of his head. Floyd now had both weapons trained on Caleb, who was sobbing uncontrollably now. Macaulay felt trapped in an episode of the *Twilight Zone* or a bad dream that he could not wake up from. But this was all too real and the continued threats from the stranger told him that his life could end at any minute.

"You'd better stop moving. Stop crying or I'm gonna shoot you," Floyd barked in a forceful, yet slow southern drawl.

"Sir, I have no weapon," Macaulay replied. "I didn't do anything wrong, I'm a passenger."

"I don't care. You tried to run me over, you tried to kill a cop." Floyd was getting even angrier now.

Caleb insisted that he wasn't responsible. "I'm the passenger," he tried to emphasize once more. "I was riding home from work, I have no clue what's going on."

Floyd applied a firm grip on both guns. "I'm gonna shoot you if you keep moving,"

"Sir, you can't shoot me, you'll be charged with murder."

Floyd let out a sinister laugh. "I'm on medication, so it doesn't matter what you have. This is the twenty-third guy I've killed." He then peered back to the Toyota Celica and the body slumped over in the driver's seat. "Oh, I shot him good," Floyd said, admiring his own work. He pulled off his white T-shirt, revealing his sizable girth and several white bandages on his back. Floyd walked to the front of the Toyota, rolled up the shirt and tried to apply a tourniquet to the bleeding officer.

The ex-Marine then began inspecting Bruce McKay's gun more thoroughly. Something wasn't working right. Caleb kept his own hands on his head, while his captor fumbled with the weapon. Caleb kept his eyes focused on the guns. One was still pointed directly at him while Floyd continued examining the other. *Is it out of bullets? Is it jammed?* These questions ran through Caleb's mind as he averted his eyes from Greg Floyd's menacing stare. Caleb couldn't look Floyd directly in the eyes or even talk to him.

When he had tried to do that, Greg Floyd only grew more agitated. Instead, the younger man wept and prayed for someone to come along and save him from this ordeal.

Joel and Connie McKenzie had no idea what was happening on the front lawn of their home or what had happened in the dirt parking lot in front of Joel's welding shop across the street. Both were returning home from a rare trip together downtown. Connie's car was getting fixed and she needed to pick up some trash bags. On the ride into the town center, they had seen Corporal Bruce McKay pull over Liko Kenney on that turnabout on Route 116. The couple had thought nothing of it at the time. On the return trip, the McKenzies were in separate vehicles. Connie was behind the wheel of her own car heading down Easton Road when she saw Liko Kenney's Toyota Celica parked up on her lawn. She pulled up on the grass in front of her house and rushed over to see what was going on and whether she could offer any assistance. After all, Connie McKenzie was a nurse.

Sam Stephenson had just left a job site in Easton where he had spent the day clearing trees with his friend Chuck Herbert. Stephenson was making his way back to his shop on Route 116 in Franconia towing heavy equipment behind his six-wheel dump truck. He had a 60-foot man-lift strapped to his 22-ton trailer. Chuck Herbert was following close behind in Stephenson's pickup truck. Sam was planning to drop the equipment off and then give Chuck a ride back to the job site where his own vehicle was waiting. Stephenson passed the Tamarack tennis courts and shifted the dump truck into fourth gear. The road was a straight line now, and with any luck he could just coast until he came upon his shop. As he was shifting into high range four, Sam looked up and noticed a gray vehicle driving across the road up ahead. It appeared that one of the vehicle's tires was off the road. Sam slowed down; as he got a little closer, he saw the Franconia police cruiser parked in the dirt lot, but there was no sign of the officer. He then spotted Liko Kenney's car across Route 116 and up on a lawn. At first glance, it appeared to be an accident. The glass in the Toyota Celica's passenger-side window had shattered and there was also some kind of crack in the windshield. Sam didn't want to add to the traffic mess, especially with all the heavy equipment he was towing. He decided to pull his dump truck into the dirt lot, hoping that he could drive behind Joel McKenzie's welding shop and back onto Route 116. But as Stephenson was turning the steering wheel, he looked down at the Toyota Celica and noticed Liko hunched over in the driver's seat, the sun shining on his reddish brown hair. Liko's head was almost touching the car door. Sam thought he was unconscious, but only that. *Maybe he cracked his head on the windshield*, he thought. He could also see that Kenney's car was on top of someone, but Sam couldn't tell who it was.

Sam's plans of bypassing the scene and getting back to his shop were over now. He slammed on the brakes, shut the truck off, and then jumped out to see what the matter was. Sam cut through a break in a stone wall and found his way onto the lawn near Liko's vehicle. Chuck Herbert had jumped out of the pickup truck and begun running toward the Toyota Celica from the other side. Stephenson took about fifteen steps toward the car and heard Greg Floyd's voice for the first time. "Stop right there. Don't come any closer." Floyd was standing by the driver's side of Liko's car and Sam could not see that the ex-Marine was holding two guns in his hands. Stephenson did notice Caleb Macaulay sitting on the ground and another young man (who he later found out was Gregory Paul Floyd). Sam recognized Caleb, but couldn't remember his name. He had never seen either of the Floyds before and he still had not grasped the full scope of what was happening here. "Hey, do you need some help getting that car off that guy?" he asked.

"Stop right there," Floyd yelled again. "Don't come any closer." Floyd came around the front of the Toyota Celica and Sam saw that he was holding two black firearms firmly in his hands; both guns were pointed down to the ground. That was enough for him to see. Stephenson turned immediately around and walked back toward his friend Chuck Herbert, who was approaching from the road.

"Chucky, hey, hey, hey. . . . Don't go any closer," Sam warned. Chucky glanced over at Floyd and understood the message. "Whoa, look out. He's got a gun."

Detective David Wentworth and patrol officer Phillip Blanchard were finally approaching the scene on Route 116 in Franconia. It had been some time since the officers had heard anything come across the police scanner. Wentworth looked ahead, hoping to see blue lights flashing or at least Bruce McKay's cruiser parked in the middle of the road. Instead, McKay's SUV was in the dirt lot off to the side. He also spotted another vehicle, this one belonging to Sugar Hill Fire Chief Allan Clark. Clark had been in the life-saving business for more than thirty years. In fact, he had been one of the first emergency medical technicians commissioned in the state of New Hampshire. He was a good man to have in a crisis, and Wentworth was relieved to have him there. There was another car just ahead of Allan Clark's vehicle parked up on a lawn on the lefthand side of Route 116. Wentworth told Blanchard to pull off to the righthand side of the road. The police sergeant got out of the cruiser and made his way toward the car on the lawn. The first person he saw was Caleb Macaulay sitting Indian style on the grass with his hands on his head about twenty feet away from the rear of the Celica. Tears were streaming down the young man's face.

"Who are you?" Wentworth asked.

"Caleb Macaulay, sir," he said between sobs.

The detective made a mental note of it and continued walking toward the light blue hatchback. *Piece of crap car*, Wentworth thought to himself. He saw the driver and assumed it was Liko Kenney. Wentworth didn't need to check for a pulse. *He's obviously dead*, he thought. Liko's skin had turned a yellowish color. His head was off to the side and both hands were down in his lap. The veteran cop then looked down toward the ground and felt his heart jump into his throat. He could see the blue pant leg of Bruce McKay's uniform sticking out from under the car.

"He's still alive," Allan Clark shouted. The Sugar Hill Fire Chief was standing in front of the car trying to determine the best course of action. This wasn't a stranger he was dealing with; this was a friend. Clark headed up the mountain search and rescue team in these parts and had worked many times with Bruce McKay. The fire chief also knew Liko Kenney, but only in passing. Ironically, just a few hours before the shooting, Liko Kenney had loaded Clark's pickup truck with fertilizer. Everyone knew everyone around here. "The people we [EMT, firemen, police officers] deal with are the people we know," Clark explained later. "It is more rewarding when you're truly helping your neighbors. I unfortunately deal with death on a regular basis. Most are hikers, crash victims, and self-inflicted gunshot wounds. You treat each victim the same, but the ones you know are the ones that stick with you. " Allan Clark had been listening to the drama unfold just moments before on his scanner. He was the first medical responder on the scene and a bit unnerved by the fact that the scene itself was not yet secure. He had asked Greg Floyd to put down his weapons but the man refused. Clark had then attended to Liko Kenney and knew immediately that he was dead. Now he was trying to save the life of a longtime colleague.

David Wentworth began making his way to Clark's position at the front of the Toyota Celica when someone else hollered, "Put down the guns!" It was his partner Phil Blanchard. Wentworth turned and saw a large, bald, shirtless man with two weapons in his hands. Greg Floyd kept both guns in his meaty palms as he stared back at Blanchard. "I said, drop the guns," the patrol officer repeated in a more forceful tone. Blanchard immediately recognized the pistol that Floyd was holding by the side in his right hand. It was a .45 caliber Sig Sauer, the same style gun that the Franconia Police Department issued its officers. "That's Bruce McKay's service weapon," Phil said to himself. Floyd was now holding the gun with his hands around the grip and the patrolman could not tell if the man's finger was inside the trigger guard or not. Blanchard's eyes followed the weapon up Floyd's right forearm and noticed a trail of blood up to his elbow.

"Drop the fucking guns," Blanchard ordered once more, but again the man didn't move. Instead, Floyd turned his bulky body around to directly face the officer. *Keep cool, just keep cool,* Blanchard thought. This was all new territory for him. Blanchard was fresh out of the police academy for part-time officers and was nearing the end of his field training programs. He had been on a few ride-alongs but had never seen or been confronted by an armed subject before. Blanchard kept his focus on Floyd's hands. He had no idea what his facial expression was at this point or even whether the man understood his commands. Still, Blanchard repeated the order two more times as sternly as he could. It was if the loud clear tenor of Blanchard's voice broke Floyd from his momentary trance. The man finally began to lower both weapons to the ground.

"Easy son," Floyd said staring up at Blanchard. "I'm quicker than you." Floyd placed both guns on the ground and was ordered by the officer to step back. Blanchard then called for another cop on the scene to stand over the two pistols.

"Has either of these weapons been secured?" the officer asked.

"No," Blanchard told him. "And don't touch either weapon." With one possible threat neutralized, Blanchard joined David Wentworth and Allan Clark to see if they could get the Toyota Celica off their dying comrade.

Corporal Bruce McKay's body was under the Toyota Celica between the tires and parallel to the front bumper; his head was on the passenger side. The full weight of the vehicle appeared to be resting on the police officer's body. "Bruce, hey Bruce," Chief Allan Clark called out. Clark looked down at McKay and thought he saw some recognition in the man's glazed eyes. Clark then reached down and placed a finger over McKay's carotid artery. He could feel a slow, weak pulse. "I think I gotta pulse," he announced. "We gotta get this car off him."

By this time, two other witnesses had arrived. Brandon Sherborn had heard shots fired and rushed to the scene with his father Stanley from their home just down the road. The Sherborns' grabbed one end of the Toyota Celica, while Detective David Wentworth and Officer Phil Blanchard grabbed the other. Together the men lifted the car off Bruce McKay's broken body and tried to push it back, but the vehicle would not budge. "It's in gear," Chief Clark quickly deduced. "We have to get it out of gear in order to roll it back." Brandon Sherborn ran over to the passenger side and reached in through broken glass and put the car in neutral. The men lifted the vehicle once more and rolled it back off Corporal McKay. David Wentworth had to put his professional instincts and concerns aside. As the lead investigator, he had just helped move evidence around. This would have been a big procedural mistake if the life of the man underneath wasn't at stake. Still, if there was a case to be prosecuted down the road, the evidence could not be jeopardized too much. As the Toyota Celica was pushed back three feet, Wentworth was somewhat relieved to see a blood stain on the grass that he could later use as an identifier as to the exact location where the vehicle would have been.

Chief Clark was now able to see Bruce McKay's body in full view. The officer had lacerations on his face and both of his legs were spread apart with one leg folded back in an unnatural position. McKay's pelvis was shattered. He also had cuts to his scalp, lower lip, and the tip of his nose had been torn off. The injuries were gruesome, but not life-threatening. Clark had been trained to pay no attention to what professionals call "distracting injuries." He had tunnel vision now and was focused on bringing back a life. Clark moved McKay's head to one side to provide a clear passageway for air. There was no blood or any other foreign materials in his mouth. This was a positive sign. "I need my medical kit, oxygen, and defibrillator," he told the Sherborns, who then rushed to Clark's vehicle and retrieved the materials.

David Wentworth stood over his friend while Chief Clark went to work. McKay had a chalky look to his face. His left eye was gray and turned over. Wentworth also saw what he believed were McKay's intestines spilling out from a rip in the man's pants. Still, Bruce McKay was taking breaths. "C'mon, Bruce," he pleaded. One onlooker was not so hopeful. "He's fucked," Greg Floyd callously observed while Allan Clark was performing CPR. Hearing this, Detective Wentworth exploded. The shock of seeing his comrade lying helplessly on the ground and the sheer magnitude of the situation caused him to boil over. *If Bruce is able to hear those words, his body is gonna shut down*, Wentworth thought. He did not want his friend to stop fighting. The detective got right into Greg Floyd's face. "Don't say that, don't you fucking say that!" he growled.

Floyd was not one to back down. "Hey, fuck you guys," he replied. "I'm tryin' to help. This is how I'm gonna get treated?" The ex-Marine continued to shout as Wentworth fought to regain his composure and finally backed off. *This isn't the time, or the place*, he thought to himself. Wentworth apologized in an attempt to diffuse the situation and also because he did not want to alienate Greg Floyd to the police. David Wentworth was tapping into his professional instincts once again. "He (Floyd) could be a real good witness for us," Wentworth explained to investigators later. "If he gets pissed off, then we're not gonna get anything out of him." The detective then told Floyd, "Look, I'm sorry. I didn't mean to light you up there. Just do me a favor. I need you to cross the road. I need you to be away from here." Wentworth explained to the man what negative effect his words could have on Bruce McKay who was still alive and undergoing CPR. "I didn't want Officer McKay to hear you say, I'm fucked, because I didn't want him to stop fighting." Floyd appeared to understand and walked back across the road toward his son and Caleb Macaulay.

Allan Clark paid no attention to the argument between Wentworth and Floyd. His only concern was Bruce McKay, whose life appeared to be quickly slipping away. Before beginning CPR, Clark had inserted an oral pharyngeal into McKay's airway. Clark noticed the officer had no gag reflex and thought, *uh oh, this isn't good.* With some help, the fire chief then attached oxygen to his bag valve mask and respirations. He was trying to breathe life back into Bruce McKay, but he was getting no response. Connie McKenzie was assisting Clark's efforts. She checked McKay's radial pulse and found none. Chief Clark would have to begin chest compressions. As he prepared the defibrillator, Clark contemplated how he was going to remove the officer's bulletproof vest, which was customarily Velcroed at the sides. *It's gonna be tricky,* he thought to himself. At that moment, Clark tore open Corporal McKay's shirt, cut off his T-shirt and was immediately taken aback. The officer was not wearing a protective vest. The discovery also puzzled David Wentworth, who knew Bruce McKay to be a safety-conscious police officer. "That's so out of character for him," Wentworth explained to investigators later. "I mean he wears his vest to court, I mean if he doesn't wear his uniform, he'll still have his vest on. . . . It just kinda blew my mind that I wasn't seeing the vest there."

Both men also recognized severe trauma to Bruce McKay's legs, especially the left pelvis area. Just above the pelvic area, he had a gaping wound on his right side below the ribs. Still, Chief Clark was forced to block these horrors out of his mind as he continued chest compressions. "Breathe, c'mon, breathe," he whispered to McKay.

It was approximately 6:15 P.M. when paramedic Amy Cyrs arrived on the scene. By this time, the crowd of police officers, EMTs, and onlookers had swelled to nearly two dozen people. Cyrs was directed into the scene as close as firefighters could allow. She parked her vehicle and ran over to the Franconia Life Squad Unit and asked colleague Evelyn Eastton what was needed. "This is a bad one," she was told. Both lifted the stretcher out of the ambulance and made their way toward Bruce McKay, lying on the grass a few feet away from the Toyota Celica. Cyrs glanced inside the car and saw the person in the driver's seat slumped to the side covered in blood. She turned her attention back to the wounded officer, who had just been placed on a backboard. Cyrs helped lift McKay's body onto the stretcher while others continued to perform CPR. The medical response personnel would not give up until Bruce McKay had let out his last breath. They loaded the stretcher into the ambulance and sped off toward Littleton Regional Hospital, eleven miles away.

After the Life Squad unit took off, another argument broke out across the street, this time between Caleb Macaulay and Greg Floyd's son. "I don't believe this is happening. I can't believe all the bullshit going on," Macaulay wailed. "I've got pepper spray in my eyes. I can't believe you shot my friend."

"You tried running over my father," Gregory Paul Floyd yelled back. "You're lucky you didn't get shot too." Officer Phil Blanchard separated the two and walked the younger Floyd and his father about twenty feet away from Macaulay. The elder Floyd was quiet, but Blanchard could tell that he was still buzzing like a bee in a hive.

"You okay?" Blanchard asked. "I'm fine, that was the forty-third person I've killed," Floyd said upping his previous death count from twenty-three. "I'm fine."

Sam Stephenson had overheard the shouting match between Gregory Paul Floyd and Caleb Macaulay and was finally able to make the connection between the heavy-set bald man with the heavy-set teenager with blond hair. Stephenson walked toward the elder Floyd and introduced himself, adding, "Thanks for not shooting." Floyd told him, "I had three, three tours in Vietnam. I'm a Marine. I didn't know who the fuck you were coming out of the woods." Stephenson asked him how the whole thing went down. "I'm a Marine," Floyd boasted once more. "I know how to use a gun. I don't know who the fuck he [Kenney] is, I dunno who the fuck is under the car, but, God damn, nobody's gonna run somebody over and just run them down, two times right there in front of me. I've been around the world and I'm not putting up with that crap."

An officer who had been standing with Floyd and his son told them to remain where they were while everything got straightened out. "I can't believe I shot him," Greg Floyd said, referring to Liko Kenney. He then turned back toward the officer, the shock and sorrow now gone. "You need to tell your friend [McKay] to get a new gun, that thing jammed on me."

At this point, Sergeant Dave Wentworth was facing a different challenge. He had to get control of the crime scene and he had to do it quickly. People were walking all over the place. *Okay, first I need to determine exactly who the witnesses are*, he thought. *Who's here and who shouldn't be here?* Wentworth, despite his experience, was feeling overwhelmed. Part of his mind was still on his friend. *Will Bruce live? Will he die?* The attention he had been paying to McKay was taking his focus away from the scene as a whole. *I gotta make up for that, I gotta get things moving.*

Wentworth was approached by one of the paramedics, who told him he would tarp the car and throw a blanket over the driver's side of the vehicle. "Okay, that's good," Wentworth replied. *The media's gonna be on its way, other witnesses; people who maybe shouldn't be seeing this kind of thing.* The EMTs threw two cloth blankets over both the driver's side and passenger side of the Toyota Celica. They were about to throw a plastic tarp over the back when Wentworth told them to hold on a minute. "Guys, I appreciate it," he said. "But I've got to think about the evidence. Is this (tarp) gonna start to affect the temperature in there and those kinds of things? Are things gonna decay?" Wentworth was also thinking about having even more people tracking their footprints around the vehicle, not to mention fingerprints when they attempted to put the tarp on. "Just leave it. Just leave the tarp," he called out. The EMTs left the tarp partially folded by the vehicle.

Wentworth had taken some photographs of his friend before he was taken away in the ambulance. He handed the camera over to Officer Blanchard to take the rest. At this point, officers from Littleton, Woodstock, and the Coos County Sheriff's department had all arrived at the crime scene. A call had also been placed to Franconia Police Chief Mark Montminy, who was attending an event for his daughter's graduation at Plymouth State College that weekend. Wentworth asked one of the officers to help him begin to separate the witnesses. "'cause at this point, I'm starting to think everybody's a witness," he later told authorities. He asked the officer to get names, addresses, and phone numbers. "I don't want 'em going anywhere. Bring 'em to one place and keep an eye on 'em."

Troopers from the New Hampshire State Police were also on the scene now and this was a big relief for Dave Wentworth. These were police officers with jurisdiction and a little more detective and crime scene experience than he had. As that transition was beginning to take place, Wentworth found himself with what could be the most difficult task of all. He was the one who would have to break the news to Bruce McKay's family.

6

Life is a game and I am the referee.

BRUCE MCKAY

Sharon Davis was heading up Route 93 from Concord with one hand on the steering wheel and the other on her cell phone. It was her "every other Friday ritual." She had just dropped off her two boys, Matthew and Michael, at their father's home and was en route to Franconia for a bite to eat with Bruce. Because he was working second shift that evening, Sharon would grab a couple of subs at Quizno's, their favorite sandwich shop in Littleton, and meet Bruce back at the police station. She had just left a lengthy voice mail message for the Reverend Lyn Winter, the minister who was going to perform their wedding ceremony at the summit of Cannon Mountain in July. The nuptials were still nearly three months away but Sharon, a typical nervous bride-to-be, wanted to go over the plans with the Reverend Winter one more time just to be clear. Sharon, like Bruce, was a detail-oriented person. They lived in worlds where details and facts mattered above all else. Sharon worked as a microbiologist and hard data had no room for emotional persuasion in her profession. The same could be said about Bruce. Rarely did he let his feelings get in the way of his police work. To McKay, the law was the law and it applied equally to everyone in his little corner of the world. He would hand a friend a speeding ticket as quickly as he would a stranger. That black-and-white attitude rubbed many folks the wrong way, but others appreciated the fact that McKay didn't play favorites.

Sharon passed Plymouth State University (formerly Plymouth State College) as she continued north on Route 93 and was puzzled by the fact that she had yet to pass a state police cruiser. This stretch of highway was usually good for two or three, especially on a Friday night in early spring and especially during graduation weekend. She was about to place her cell phone back inside her purse when it suddenly rang. *Boy, the Reverend is certainly quick to answer a voice mail,* she thought to herself. "Hello?"

"Where are you?" The voice wasn't Reverend Lyn Winter. The voice belonged to Franconia Police Sergeant Mark Taylor.

"I'm heading up 93," Sharon replied. "I'm going to have dinner with Bruce. Why?"

"Come directly to Littleton Hospital," he told her. A feeling of dread covered Sharon Davis' body like a blanket as she took her foot slowly off the gas pedal, her heart pounding. "Please tell me if Bruce is alive or dead," she screamed into the cell phone. Sergeant Taylor would not give her an answer. Instead, he repeated the request to head directly to the hospital.

Norman Bruce McKay's long, winding road to the North Country had begun forty-eight years earlier and 298 miles away, in New York. He was born in the village of Bronxville on November 6, 1958. His parents, Norman Bruce, Sr., and Catherine (Hoffman) McKay were native New Yorkers who had met during a lifesaving class in high school and had continued to date while in college. Bruce's father studied art and music at Union College in Schenectady while his mother attended Green Mountain Junior College in Poultney, Vermont. The two appeared to be a perfect fit for one another despite their obvious differences. Bruce was a nonpracticing Presbyterian who lived by the simple motto: "Being good is good enough." Catherine, on the other hand, was a devout Roman Catholic who had made Bruce Sr. promise to raise their children by the teachings of her faith before accepting his hand in marriage. As religion wasn't a big deal for Bruce Sr., he gave in to the demand without protest. The couple married right out of college and migrated to southwest Texas, where Bruce Sr. completed his military service as an army medic at Fort Sam Houston in San Antonio.

The McKays remained in the area following Bruce's discharge. He was hired as a guest lecturer at the University of Texas and was beginning to make a name for himself in the local art world, thanks in part to his mentor Cecil Casebier. Cecil Lang Casebier was a cofounder of the Men of the Art Guild and would later be known for his breathtaking semi-abstract design based on the Apostles' Creed on the stained-glass windows of St. Luke's Episcopal Church in San Antonio. Casebier opened several artistic doors for the young McKay and had even approached him about taking a curator position at the prestigious Whitte Museum should one open up. At the time in 1958, the Whitte Museum boasted vast collections of ethnographic art and historic artifacts from the rugged Trans-Pecos region of South Texas. Opportunity was abundant for the McKays in San Antonio, but Catherine had her doubts. She was now pregnant with Bruce Jr. and was wary about raising her children there. There were approximately 260,000 Catholics living in San Antonio in the late 1950s; that is, only 35.8 percent of the population. Roman Catholics were a minority and provided an easy target for some. "When the economy went south, Catholics were the first ones in San Antonio to lose their jobs," Bruce McKay, Sr., recalls. "My wife didn't believe any children of ours would receive a fair shake so we packed up and headed back east to New York."

Once back home, Bruce McKay, Sr., would be forced to make another sacrifice, giving up a career in art for the better pay and security of a career in the textiles industry. The McKay family eventually settled in Locust Valley in the heart of Long Island's fabled Gold Coast, where publishing tycoon Frank Doubleday and industrialist Myron Taylor had once made their homes. The town itself is made up of dense woods, rolling hills, and exclusive country clubs. The McKays weren't rich, but they were comfortably middle class. The family lived on the site of an old estate that had been divided over time. There was a mansion, a carriage house, and several other small buildings supporting it. Bruce Sr. had purchased what was once the gardener's house, tucked away in the forest along a road not frequently traveled. It offered the perfect environment for his energetic and inquisitive son, who spent his childhood days exploring the woods, chasing after animals, and always getting muddy. It was a "Beaver Cleaver" way of life, where a child's only fears came from his closet and the local movie house. Like their neighbors, the McKays did not have to lock their doors at night and did not need to keep a watchful eye over their son.

Young Bruce was thus free to roam the environs, feeding his curiosity while gaining a true appreciation of the outdoors. He was reared primarily by his mother, who encouraged his sense of adventure. "I wasn't around a lot while Bruce was a child," Bruce McKay, Sr., admits. "I do remember that Bruce was a particularly happy kid though." He was a happy and protective child, especially when his younger sister Meggen arrived eight years later. Because of the age difference, theirs was not a typical sibling relationship. Bruce watched over Meggen as a mother bear would her cub. "Bruce ran to my defense when my father spanked me once," she recalls. "He told my father: don't ever spank my sister again. That's not right." The difference between wrong and right were lines that could not be blurred in the young man's eyes. Bruce Sr. found this out when he and Catherine decided to split up when their son was a teenager. "We just grew apart," Bruce Sr. says of the breakup with Catherine. "Like many people who find themselves in a divorce, we got married too early and before we knew who we were." The father tried to explain this to his son but young Bruce refused to listen. He was angry at his father but didn't have the means of expressing that anger with words. "He kept a lot of things bottled up inside of him," McKay Sr. explains. Bruce helped his father move into a new apartment in New York City and returned quickly to his mother and sister on Long Island. "Bruce and I grew apart after that," the father says sadly.

Bruce the boy was quickly becoming a man and his strength and coordination were growing by the day. Unlike most teenagers of the early 1970s, he was vehemently opposed to drug use of any kind. "Dope's for dopes," he would lecture his younger sister. Instead of spending his time philosophizing with friends in the back of a smoke-filled van, Bruce was a fair-haired Johnny Weissmuller, patrolling the local beach as a lifeguard. He didn't have the build of a Weissmuller, though; Bruce was not broadly muscled. But he was lean and deceptively strong. His physical skills were also displayed on the athletic fields of the Portledge School, a private institution where he played lacrosse and captained the soccer team as a fearless goalie. "He was the big man on campus," Meggen McKay-Payerle remembers. "He was very handsome, the guy all the girls wanted to date, but he was also very humble and if he saw something wrong, he was the first one to jump in and try to help." That valiant attitude nearly cost Bruce his life on the night of his high school graduation in 1977. "Bruce was walking on the beach with a girl when a group of kids started some trouble," Meggen explains. The trouble quickly escalated to an all-out brawl and one teen hit Bruce with a baseball bat or a two by four on the side of his head, cracking the membrane around his brain. "My brother was seriously injured and always had to protect his head after that." He did not, however, swear off physical action. Bruce drove a motorcycle around town and continued to push his body with marathon hikes through the dense Long Island woods.

After graduating high school, Bruce enrolled at the University of New England in Henniker, New Hampshire, where he studied environmental engineering. McKay was a good student but spent more of his time outside the classroom and in the wild. He was something of a pioneer in the days before extreme sports became the rage. Bruce hired himself out as a guide for adventure seekers and would accompany them to remote areas in northern New England and Canada where they would get dropped off by helicopter and spend the next several days living off the land. "Bruce was good with a bow and arrow and knew what to eat off trees," his father remembers. "He was a real survivor."

Bruce also proved to be a real survivor in his first marriage. As his father had done, he married a girl right out of college. It was another case of opposites attract, and like his parents' marriage this was too was doomed from the start. Ramona Belenger was even quieter than Bruce was. "She was a woman who would have been more comfortable living in the 1870s," claims Bruce Sr. "She was very plain and very demure. I didn't see any spark between them." Religion was also important to Ramona Belenger. Bruce had been raised Catholic by his devout mother but had chosen to become a Quaker when he married Ramona. Bruce McKay's foray into married life mirrored his father's in other ways as well. He too was forced to give up his passion for the security of a steady paycheck. Bruce Sr. was surprised when his son told him that he was following in his footsteps for a career in textiles. Bruce began working for J.C. Penney and then landed a job as a sweater buyer for L.L. Bean. He also spent time selling insurance and financial planning. He spent ten years married to Ramona trying to be the ideal husband while grappling with a loss of identity. It is possible that Bruce stayed in an unhappy marriage far too long because he wanted to prove to his father that it was an institution worth fighting for. The cornerstone of that institution was children and that's where he could not pretend that everything was all right between Ramona and him. Bruce desperately wanted children. He wanted a child to explore with; he wanted a child to teach and love. Ramona did not want children and, despite her reserved attitude, refused to acquiesce to his request. Bruce McKay now felt he had to walk away. The breakup with Ramona was quiet and amiable, much as their relationship had been.

Bruce was divorced for three years before meeting his second wife, Angela Somers, and it was during this period that he finally found his calling. Actually, he had found his calling years ago but this was the first time he had acted upon it. He moved up to the Franconia area and got a job as a buyer with Littleton Stamp and Coin, a small company that sold ancient Roman coins, pre–Civil

War U.S. pennies and the occasional Confederate note. It may have been another sales job, but it provided him with enough free time to pursue his true passion: public service. Bruce completed a twelve-week course at the New Hampshire police academy and was hired as a part-time police officer with the town of Haverhill, New Hampshire. His critics might say Bruce lusted for authority, for a badge that would allow him to push people around, but Bruce had been an emergency medical technician since his days in high school and his commitment to helping people was pure, especially in the beginning. While on the job he met Angela, who worked as a secretary with the Haverhill Police Department. The two had similar interests; most important to Bruce was that Angela also wanted children. While Bruce's marriage to Ramona may have been short on passion and excitement, his relationship with Angela was volcanic, fiery, and potentially dangerous. "Angela was hell on wheels," Bruce McKay, Sr., says about his former daughter-in-law. He claims Angela was physically abusive toward his son. Bruce's father believes Angela's alleged anger toward his son was compounded by the fact that he wouldn't put their small Cape Cod–style home in Landaff, New Hampshire, in her name. Despite the father's assertion that his son was the victim in this relationship, it was Bruce who found himself on the receiving end of a restraining order, which Angela later surrendered. Still, he was forced into counseling but allowed to keep his badge.

Bruce McKay later joined the Franconia Police Department as a part-time officer and in 1996 was promoted to full-time status. The department was small; its headquarters a tiny space a little bigger than a phone booth along Profile Road that was shared by the town's fire department. The police station is in a narrow corner on the left side of the building. There are a couple of desks, some files, and not much else. Andy Griffith had more to work with in the fictional town of Mayberry. Franconia's police chief Mark Montminy relied on only three full-time officers, including McKay, to patrol the vast mountainous area of Franconia Notch. Bruce McKay took to the job with unabashed relish and, according to townsfolk, made three times as many police stops as his two colleagues (Chief Montminy did not keep any record of police stops and arrests sub-divided by the three officers). When McKay wasn't patrolling the streets in his town-issued police cruiser, he rode around in his Nissan 4×4 equipped with a vanity plate that read GOTCHA.

A big part of a police officer's job in the North Country is to protect residents from wildlife. In 1999, McKay responded to a late-night break-in at a local nursing home. The perpetrator had crashed through a window and into a resident's room. When McKay arrived on the scene, the perp was long gone but there was some evidence left behind. "I saw tufts of hair on the floor," McKay wrote in his report the next day. "I'm pretty sure it was a moose." On another occasion, a wild turkey flew into McKay's police cruiser while he was out on patrol.

Bruce had fulfilled part of his dream—he now had a daughter, Courtney, and a job he loved. Despite two bad marriages, he hadn't given up the hope that he would one day find his soul mate. Like millions of single adults, he believed the Internet could lead him on the path toward true love. He posted an advertisement on Yahoo Personals, including a few photos and a description of himself. He received a couple of nibbles here and there but one personal ad stood out from the rest. He read Sharon Davis's profile and discovered someone who was down-to-earth, loved children, and was around the same age as him. Bruce wrote her a brief e-mail, hit Send, and hoped for the best.

By rights, Sharon Davis should never have gotten the message. She had all but given up on online dating. The blonde micro-biologist had dated a couple of guys from Yahoo Personals, but those encounters didn't work out. She hadn't been dating for six months and thought she'd successfully deleted her personal ad from the Web site. Sharon was surprised when she was notified about Bruce's e-mail to her. "The message was very general, but it was also very cute," she says. "He wrote that he lived up in the mountains. Bruce didn't know that I also lived here in New Hampshire." In order to reply to the e-mail, Sharon had to pay a $50 fee to rejoin the Web site. She wrote him back and the two connected right away. Their first telephone conversation lasted for five and a half hours. "It was like we had known each other all our lives. We just had a knack for being able to communicate with each other." Sharon believes serendipity also played a role. "I was in a bad accident when I was nineteen years old. Someone had run me right off the road and into a tree. I don't remember much about it, but Bruce recalled that he was one of the EMTs who had transferred me between hospitals." The pair chatted on the phone several times before deciding to meet for a date. Bruce drove down to Concord and picked Sharon up from work. The bond they had built up on the phone spilled over in the parking lot of Police Standards and Training in Concord when Bruce stepped out of his truck, strode briskly toward her, and kissed her passionately on the lips. The move startled Sharon, but she wasn't put off by it. "I liked it," she says. "I certainly felt the same way about him." Bruce drove Sharon across New Hampshire to the Maine coast where they walked the beach and had lunch at a popular seaside restaurant. The easy rapport continued over lunch and both quickly realized that they had to look no further for love. They had found it, or it had found them.

Indeed, their only difference appeared to be their choice of decadent sweets. Sharon craved chocolate while Bruce had a weakness for black licorice jelly beans. McKay had a bigger weakness for his daughter, Courtney. "She was the epitome of daddy's little girl. She adored Bruce and clung to him, following him around everywhere he went," Sharon says. Bruce was also very cautious about bringing another woman into the tiny world he had built with his daughter. "The first time I met Courtney, she was riding on the back of Bruce's motorcycle down the Kancamagus Highway and I was following in my car," Sharon recalls. "We stopped at a beautiful spot called Beaver Pond and Bruce asked Courtney permission to give me a kiss. That's the way he was, a true gentleman." Blending a family is never easy but the new dynamic was met with more than mere acceptance from Courtney and Sharon's two boys. "Matthew and Michael loved Courtney and became her protective big brothers," says their mother. In turn, Bruce offered her sons a sense of structure and paternal values they had not really experienced growing up. On a typical evening, the McKay-Davis clan could be found all cuddled up on the couch watching an action movie. "Bruce loved cops and robbers movies and would cover my eyes during the violent parts," Sharon recalls.

Bruce rarely spoke about the real-life violence he had encountered while on the job. Sharon got the first real sense of her boyfriend's life behind the badge while the two were shopping at a Wal-Mart in Littleton, New Hampshire. "We were at the register when I could *feel* someone staring at me," Sharon says. "I turned around and saw this man looking at me. I had never seen such a look of anger and evil before." She instinctively grabbed Bruce's arm. "That guy freaks me out," she whispered. McKay gazed over and spotted Liko Kenney at the next register attempting to stare him down. "That's Bode Miller's cousin, Liko Kenney," he told Sharon. "I'll tell you about him later."

Bruce and Sharon paid for their goods and walked out to the parking lot while Liko Kenney walked ahead. The young man got into his car, his eyes focused once again on the couple. He started the vehicle, revved the engine, and pulled out right in front of the pair before tearing out of the parking lot. As Bruce drove Sharon back to his home in Landaff, he described his previous run-in with Liko Kenney. "He was very matter-of-fact about it," Sharon says. "I didn't sense any animosity on Bruce's part." McKay told Sharon that Liko Kenney had "psychological issues." While the officer didn't consider Liko Kenney much of a threat, his girlfriend certainly did. Sharon's fear of the intense young man was coupled by the fact that the back door of Bruce's house did not have a lock on it. She spent much of her time alone in the home while Bruce was at work. "I have a great fear of guns, but I was so scared of this guy that I had Bruce teach me how to use one of his pistols," Sharon remembers. The initial lesson that evening was over before it had begun, however. As Bruce inspected the weapon to make sure it wasn't loaded, Sharon had dissolved into a puddle of tears while sitting on the bed. McKay put the gun away, sat down beside her, and hugged her. "Don't worry, everything's gonna be okay," he whispered. Something in the back of Sharon Davis's mind told her that he would not be able to keep that promise.

7

*I don't have to do what people say
just because they're being bossy.*

LIKO KENNEY

January 26, 2003

The sky was black, the air bitterly cold, and a light snow had begun falling softly over Franconia Notch. The thick white flakes danced sideways across the headlights of Bruce McKay's patrol vehicle. The evening had been quiet thus far but McKay knew this was about to change. It was Super Bowl Sunday after all. The New England Patriots weren't playing in the big game this year but there were plenty of Oakland Raider fans in these parts. At this moment, Al Davis's team was getting trampled by the Tampa Bay Buccaneers at Qualcomm Stadium in San Diego. Here in the North Country the Super Bowl parties were in full swing and because of the lopsided score most fans had no doubt become less interested in the game and more focused on getting drunk. *It's gonna be a long night,* McKay thought to himself. He was driving along Dow Avenue in Franconia when he spotted a single set of fresh tire tracks on the snow-covered road leading to Fox Hill Park. McKay knew the area was popular among teenagers who gathered there to drink and smoke pot. The officer pulled off Dow Avenue and followed the tire tracks into the parking lot of Fox Hill Park where he noticed a white Subaru Loyale parked in the darkness with its lights off. It appeared to be empty. McKay shined a spotlight on the back of the vehicle and wrote down the license plate number: NH 625447. He radioed into dispatch and was informed that the car belonged to Michele Kenney of Easton. McKay took his eyes off the license plate and began inspecting the area around the vehicle. *No fresh footprints,* he thought. *Whoever was in the car must still be in there.*

It also didn't appear to the officer that the vehicle had been there long. The Subaru wasn't running but the falling snow had yet to accumulate on the windows. The windows weren't frosted over, either, despite the bone-chilling midwinter temperature of 14 degrees Fahrenheit. McKay stepped out of his police SUV and approached the vehicle with his high-powered flashlight held high in his right hand. He shined the light through the driver's-side window and noted the driver (later identified as Liko Kenney) was reclined in his seat. McKay tapped on the glass and Liko rolled down the window. The officer explained to him that there had been suspicious activity in the area and that he was just checking to see what was going on. Kenney told McKay that he was only relaxing as he waited for some friends to arrive from a Super Bowl party. The explanation made no sense to the officer. The game was at halftime, and although the Buccaneers were holding a commanding 20-3 lead over the Raiders, McKay doubted Liko's friends would be leaving their party any time soon, with two quarters of football still left to play.

The officer pondered this thought as he returned to his squad car to fetch his winter coat. Liko turned the ignition and started the car. McKay returned quickly and was about to ask Kenney to shut off the engine when Liko agitatedly cut him off: "I was just wondering what your name was?" McKay was clearly startled by the driver's abruptness but remained calm: "And yours is?" "Does it matter?" Liko shot back. "Yah, do you have your driver's license handy?" McKay asked.

Liko was content to answer every question with a question. He repeatedly asked the officer why he needed his license. McKay told Liko that he was in a suspicious place at a suspicious time. Liko still refused to budge. "How am I at a suspicious place at a suspicious time?" he asked. McKay kept his cool while attempting to explain the situation. "What law says I *have* to tell you my name?" Liko pressed once more.

McKay calmly reminded the agitated young man that the New

Hampshire state driver's license exam stated that a driver operating a motor vehicle was required to identify him- or herself upon request. Liko argued that he wasn't *operating* the car and that he had only turned it on to stay warm. "You started the car, it's operated. It's operated," McKay pointed out. Liko finally realized that he only had two choices. He could produce his license and registration or he could spend the rest of his Sunday night in jail. Liko chose the former and handed over his papers.

A flash of recognition came over McKay as he studied the name on the laminated identification card: Liko Kenney, 228 Easton Valley Rd. Easton, New Hampshire 03580. Date of Birth: 04/26/83. "Ah, I was wondering why you had such an attitude," McKay told him. The officer had never met Liko before but certainly knew him by reputation. The officer returned to his patrol car for a moment while Liko stepped out of the Subaru Loyale. "Can I have my license back now?" Kenney hollered as he stood by the driver's side door.

Bruce McKay kept his eye on Liko as he radioed dispatch. "44-K Grafton."

"44-K, go ahead," the dispatcher replied.

"Clear to copy for a New Hampshire 21." At this moment, Liko Kenney began marching toward the police car. McKay took his thumb off the radio and shouted out the window: "Get back in your car, Liko."

"Why?"

"'Cause I told you to. Do it now!"

"I don't have to do what people say just because they're being bossy," Liko whined.

Bruce McKay had had enough. "Hey, get in your car or you'll sit in mine," he ordered, his voice showing the first signs of anger. "I'm giving you a lawful order to get back in your car now. You're on video and you're on audio . . . if you want to pursue it . . ."

Liko's protest was now becoming dangerous. The young man continued to bait McKay, saying that he had a right to be standing outside the patrol car. "You will get in your car or you will sit in mine in handcuffs!" the officer reiterated. Liko Kenney still wouldn't budge. Instead he continued to talk about his right to be in a public place and his right to know what the police officer was doing with his driver's license. McKay then suggested that Liko go back to school and find out what his rights really were. "Don't I have a right to know what you're doing with my property? I do know my rights!" Kenney countered. "Why are you harassing me, man? Can I ask you?"

Corporal McKay got out of his vehicle and reached for Liko's arm. "Put your hands around your back," he ordered as Liko struggled to break free. "Do not touch me," the young man warned. "Do not put your hands on me! I'm asking you a simple question."

"Get in the fucking car and do it now!" the officer said, reaching for Liko once again.

"Do not touch my arm! Do not put your hands on me!" Liko screamed as he saw McKay reaching for the container of pepper spray on his belt. "Do not even think about *that*!"

"Oh yes, Liko!" the officer replied.

"I'll take you to court and sue you for harassment charges. What are you doing? I'm simply asking you when I can have my license back."

"I'm giving you a direct order to get into your car!"

"You can't stir people around. You're not *fucking God*! Why are you giving me an order? You have no reason order me around!"

At this point, McKay knew that it was best not to handle Liko Kenney alone, so he called for backup—to which Liko Kenney agreed, saying that he felt harassed. Liko then demanded that McKay to give him his license back. Of course, McKay refused the request, explaining that Kenney wasn't complying with his order. "You should be sitting in the back of my car right now!"

"Complying with your orders? You're not here to order people around. You're here to serve and protect!" McKay agreed and explained that he was protecting the public by investigating a suspicious car parked in the middle of nowhere. Once more, Liko Kenney refused to cooperate and questioned the officer for grabbing his arm. "Why do police officers go down the street beatin' kids up?" McKay, looking for a quick exit to this marathon argument, reached for his pepper spray. Liko kept his eyes on the officer's hands. "What, you gonna spray me with pepper spray? You'd *better* spray me with pepper spray!"

"If it comes to that," McKay warned holding the container in a firm grip.

Liko threatened to sue the officer, to which McKay reminded him that his patrol car was rolling videotape on the entire incident and that he was confident that anyone who viewed it would see who the real agitator was. "You can go and steal stuff from people, put your hands on people, give people orders," Liko charged. "Who gives you the right to do this? This is a free country! You don't have a right to harass me!"

"I recommend that you go sit back in your car," McKay said once again.

"I recommend that you give me my license back because I'm driving home."

"You're not going anywhere right now!"

Liko warned McKay that if he got back into his car, "I'm driving home." Liko returned to his mother's Subaru and made good on his promise. He started the engine and slammed the vehicle in reverse as the front tires kicked off the falling snow. Bruce McKay also returned to his squad car and radioed dispatch. "We're currently off where the suspicious subject has now elected to turn hostile." McKay sat alone in his cruiser watching Liko as he attempted to flee. "You should be advised that the party is attempting to leave. He's not gonna get outta here but he's attempting to leave." Bruce McKay backed up his cruiser, blocking the only exit to Fox Hill Park.

Liko pulled his car up to the front grill of the cruiser and then quickly backed up again. Like a wild mustang, Liko drove his car around the small parking area spinning his wheels and looking for a way out. Both he and McKay knew this was a futile exercise. Liko was trapped. Realizing this, he parked his car and got out again. Liko demanded once more that another police officer be called to the scene. McKay, who remained in his squad car, told him that other officers were on the way. Liko then did something that was uncharacteristic for the young rebel he claimed to be. "I have to be somewhere. . . . I have to be back with my mom's car. You're preventing me from leaving. You have my license right there. Why don't you give me my license and let me go home instead of doing this?" Liko had dropped the James Dean attitude; he was now playing a typical American teen who was worried about returning home late with his parents' car. When this strategy didn't work, Liko reverted back to his defiant stance. "You're torturing me. Why are you torturing me? Why are you tormenting me? Can't you go arrest a drunk at a bar or something? Why? Why are you bothering me?" Liko continued to request that another officer be called in while McKay remained silent. The time for talking was over. The officer knew now that Kenney was beyond reasoning with. Liko continued his harangue without interruption as the sound of the police sirens grew louder in the distance.

"Is that officer coming here?"

"Oh, yes," McKay answered breaking his silence.

"They'd better be coming here," Liko shot back. What the young man failed to realize was that the evening was about to get a whole lot worse for him.

Sergeant Richard Ball of the Bethlehem, New Hampshire, Police Department and Officer Steve Cox of the nearby Littleton Police Department arrived on the scene moments later, much to the relief of Bruce McKay *and* Liko Kenney. "Hello, can I please get some assistance?" Liko sighed. "This officer here [*pointing at McKay*] is harassing me. He won't answer any of my questions I've been asking him. He took my license."

Ball, Cox and McKay moved quickly toward Liko. "Put your hands on the car," McKay ordered.

"Stop touching me, please do not touch me!" Kenney cried. "I do not trust this man [*again referring to McKay*]. Please keep him away from me. . . . I haven't done anything." This time, his request was not met. Bruce McKay grabbed Liko by the hair and then by the hood of his sweatshirt and pulled him forward while the other two officers tried desperately to pin the young man's arms back. "Stop touching me! Let go of me! My neck! I have a broken neck!" Liko screamed as the four men fell forward behind his car. "Stop resisting. Stop resisting," McKay shouted. "Stop it!" Liko let out a guttural scream as he tried to fight free. "Somebody help me! I'm being molested! These officers are torturing me; these officers are trying to kill me!"

Officer Cox tried in vain to handcuff Liko, but he struggled free and staggered to the rear of his mother's car. Sergeant Ball then tripped Liko over his left leg and brought him to the ground. "You're hurting my neck!" Liko screamed once more. Officer Cox was now down near the young man's legs, while McKay placed his right knee on Kenney's head hoping to stabilize him long enough for Cox to secure the handcuffs. At this moment, Liko reached up with his right hand and squeezed McKay's testicles. The officer let out a loud scream of his own and drove his fist into the left side of Liko's face, hoping the young man would release the viselike grip on his manhood. "Don't grab my balls again!"

The blow dazed Kenney, who immediately dropped his hand. Officer Cox slapped a cuff on Liko's left hand and then the right. But Liko Kenney was not done fighting. Somehow he managed to scurry under his mother's car. Fighting his own pain, McKay grabbed Liko's boots and, with the help of Officer Cox, pulled him out from under the car. "What the fuck are you doing?" Liko wailed between screams. While Cox and Ball corralled Liko, McKay tried to walk off his injury, taking deep breaths as he bent at the waist. "He grabbed my balls," a shocked Bruce McKay told his comrades. After a few painful moments, McKay got his second wind and grabbed a pair of leg restraints from Sergeant Ball.

Liko stepped back as McKay moved toward him. "What are you gonna do with those? Stick that up my ass?"

"I'm gonna put it around your feet because I don't think you're gonna be terribly cooperative," McKay told him. "You haven't been cooperative for the whole thing."

"What the hell are you doing this for? You have no right to fucking do this to people. . . . What are you doing to me? Gonna take me out and fucking kill me somewhere?" Liko continued screaming obscenities as his feet were secured. The officers then carried Liko to McKay's police cruiser, where they had a difficult time putting him in. Liko kept his body straight as a board and tried to hook his feet under the rear door as the men tried to squeeze him inside. All the while, Liko kept talking about police harassment, police torture, and his hurting neck. Every time the officers would touch him, the young man howled in pain. Finally, Liko was wedged into the cruiser and a seat belt was placed around his upper body.

"Should we take off the seat belt in order to pull him farther into the car?" Sergeant Ball asked McKay. The officer, now exhausted, humiliated, and in pain, said no. He was fearful that Liko would cause damage to the vehicle if he wasn't strapped in. While the men decided the best course of action, Liko Kenney somehow managed to unhook his seat belt and slip out of the cruiser undetected. He attempted to hop away like an oversized rabbit in his leg restraints but did not get very far. McKay ran after him once more and threw Liko to the ground.

A New Hampshire State Trooper arrived shortly thereafter per Liko's request, but the young man paid little notice. His anger had been building steadily over the course of the incident and it had reached hysterical proportions now. Liko continued his mono-syllabic rant as he was placed in an ambulance and taken to Littleton Regional Hospital for a physical and mental evaluation. Liko had been asked by Officer Cox if he had been taking any medication; he replied that he'd been taking medicine for depression. There was no trace of liquor on Liko's breath, but Cox believed he was high on *something*. A search of Liko's mother's white Subaru uncovered a multicolored glass pipe and marijuana residue under the driver's seat. Also found in the car was an empty plastic holder for .22 caliber ammunition. As Liko was being transported to the hospital, medical technicians made another disturbing discovery; he had been hiding two knives in his pockets.

Once he arrived at the hospital, Liko continued claims of gross mistreatment. this time accusing members of the medical staff of torturing him. "Why am I being tortured?" he shouted in the emergency room. "I'm an American!" After about fifteen minutes, Liko finally calmed down long enough for State Trooper Jonathan H. Stephens to remove his handcuffs. The attending physician, Dr. Campbell McLaren found swelling and redness on Liko's wrists where the handcuffs had been applied. He also found slight swelling and tenderness on the left side of Liko's jaw (Liko and his family would later claim that McKay had broken his jaw). Dr. McLaren found the young man's neck to be pain-free. Trooper Stephens photographed Liko's face, wrists, and feet and then advised him of his Miranda rights, which he refused to waive. The time now was 11:30 P.M., three hours after the incident had begun to mushroom at Fox Hill Park. The volatile Liko had grown quiet now. He stared into Trooper Stephens eyes and said, "Will you shoot me?"

"No," a startled Stephens replied.

"Well, I guess I'll just have to kill myself."

Davey and Michele Kenney arrived at the hospital an hour later. Liko wept in his father's arms and then proceeded to tell *his* version of the story to his parents. He was released on $2,000 bail to the custody of Davey and Michele. Officer Bruce McKay drove back to the Franconia Police Department, still sore from the night's ordeal. He typed up the following complaints:

Simple Assault — The defendant (Liko Kenney) did commit the crime of Simple Assault by knowing [*sic*] causing unprivileged physical contact with the Uniformed Police Officer by grabbing the person of that Officer by the testicles with his right hand and squeezing, that Officer being that of Officer McKay of the Franconia Police Department.

Obstructing Government Administration — The defendant did commit the crime of Obstructing Government Administration in that he did knowingly use intimidation with the purpose to interfere with the public servant performing an official function, by disregarding the instructions from Officer McKay, a uniformed Police Officer of the Franconia Police Department, to stay with or return to his vehicle during an investigation of the Defendant with the Defendant exiting the vehicle, walking up to the open driver's side door of the marked Franconia patrol unit, demanding the return of his driver's license in a manner that caused said Officer concern for his safety.

Arrest of Detention — The Defendant did commit the crime of Resisting Arrest or Detention by knowingly physically interfering with Officer McKay, a uniformed Officer with the Franconia Police Department, who was at the time attempting to effect an physical arrest or detention of the defendant, by pulling free of the officer's grasp, said Defendant, by pulling free of the Officer's grasp, said Defendant recognizing the officer to [be] a Law Enforcement official.

Escape — The defendant did commit the crime of Escape while after being arrested by Officer McKay of the Franconia Police Department, placed in handcuffs and leg restraints then seated and secured by way of a seat belt in the rear of the Franconia cruiser did then undo the seatbelt and escape out the rear cruiser door which he had kept open with his feet and attempted to hop away.

Arrest or Detention — The defendant did commit the crime of Resisting Arrest or Detention by knowingly physically interfering with persons he recognized to be Law Enforcement Officials effecting a physical arrest of his person by attempting to break free of the collective hold of Officer McKay of the Franconia Police Department, Officer Cox of the Littleton Police Department and Sgt. Ball of the Bethlehem Police Department.

Acts Prohibited — The defendant did commit the violation of Acts Prohibited by having in his possession a drug preparation containing a controlled drug, to wit, a glass smoking device containing marijuana resin, in a motor vehicle under his control, to wit, a 1988 Subaru Loyale bearing New Hampshire Registration 625447.

Liko Kenney was arraigned on the charges on February 21, 2003, and was indicted by a grand jury a month later. On April 21, 2003, Kenney was ordered to pay $2000 personal recognizance bail before being released to the custody of his mother Michele Kenney.

Liko's bail was revoked six days later on April 27, 2003, thanks to a call made to the police by his uncle, Bill Kenney. The elder Kenney expressed outrage because his nephew had been riding a four-wheel ATV on what he believed was *his* property. Bill and Liko had been butting heads over the area since a similar incident in December 2002. Bill had grown frustrated by the sight of Liko racing his all-terrain vehicle up and down a long winding path on the family property known as the Kinsman Trail. "Liko liked to ride on the trail, but he never lifted a finger to maintain it and clean it up," Bill Kenney claims. Finally, the uncle took matters in his own hands and cut down a large tree to block Liko's entrance to the trail. Bill Kenney says he should have known that his nephew would not take this affront quietly. Liko simply cut down another tree and regained access to the trail. This stubborn spectacle dragged on until Liko upped the ante. Bill's Kyrgyzstanian wife, Larisa, had just awakened from an afternoon nap when she heard the roar of a chainsaw right outside the couple's cabin. Larisa rushed over to an upstairs window and peered outside where she spotted her nephew Liko with a chainsaw in both hands taking down a nearby tree. Seconds later, that tree came crashing down on the cabin. Larisa Kenney was rocked by the noise, which sounded like a bomb going off. Quickly regaining her composure, she climbed down the ladder from the second floor, grabbed her Kodak Max disposable camera and pushed open the front door. Larisa managed to snap two photos before Liko spotted her out of the corner of his eye. He rushed toward his aunt, stopping her near the door. In the panic of the moment, she grabbed a coat but hadn't had the time to put on her shoes and now she was outside the cabin standing on the ice with just a pair of socks on. Larisa raced up the front steps and quickly tossed the camera down into the cellar.

"Where is the camera?" Liko screamed as he followed her to the cabin. "Where is the camera?"

Larisa yelled back as she tried to push him away from her. "Don't touch me," Liko warned as he grabbed Larisa and pushed her back inside the cabin. Standing on the threshold of the cabin, Liko grabbed the front door and slammed it just inches from Larisa's face. The woman waited inside a few minutes for her wild nephew to leave. She heard no more noises coming from outside the cabin, so she decided to run to her sister-in-law Jo's cabin for help. As Larisa made her way outside, she heard the distinct purr of Liko's ATV coming up behind her. She headed for a big rock near her cabin, a spot she knew his all-terrain vehicle could not reach. Liko jumped off the machine and ran toward her again. "Where is the camera?" he hollered once more.

Larisa did not answer. Instead, she continued running toward the tree line while her nephew gave chase. Larisa reached her in-law's home and was pulled inside to safety while Liko turned around and headed for his parents' cabin.

Later a Kenney family summit was called between Davey and

Bill Kenney inside Bill's cabin. Liko stood outside while the two clan elders argued over what had just transpired and the question over rights to the Kinsman Trail. The heated discussion ended at an impasse and Larisa later filed a formal restraining order against her nephew. Bill Kenney's resentment toward Liko continued for several months, culminating in his call to the Franconia Police on April 27, 2003.

Corporal Bruce McKay and two other officers answered the call that evening and found Liko Kenney and his friend Alex Jackson crossing Route 116 on his way back to Liko's parents' cabin. As an officer confronted Liko, McKay noticed that the young man was transporting a blowgun with quills of steel shaft darts strapped with bungee cords to a rack in the front of his four-wheeler. McKay did not inquire about the blow gun and instead issued a warning to Liko and Jackson for not crossing the road at a 90-degree angle. Once back at the station, McKay reviewed Liko Kenney's bail conditions set forth on April 21. The pretrial order of release stated that Kenney could have no possession of a firearm or other dangerous weapon. "I believe that a blowgun equip[ped] with steel shafted darts would qualify as an 'other dangerous weapon,'" McKay later wrote, in an attempt to revoke Kenney's bail. A judge granted McKay's request, revoking Kenney's bail in June 2003 and placing him under house arrest. The punishment was upgraded less than a week later when the Grafton County Department of Corrections received a strap sever alarm indicating Liko Kenney had tampered with an electronic monitoring bracelet that had been strapped to his leg. The Department of Corrections issued an immediate order for Liko to report to the county jail. When the young man showed up with his father, he was holding the electronic bracelet in his hand. Liko then refused to be searched or to be taken to a cell. His belligerent behavior lasted several minutes before he finally complied. A month later, Liko's court-appointed attorney, Robin Warren, presented evidence to suggest that the blowgun had not belonged to Liko Kenney. Liko's companion

Alex Jackson claimed the blowgun was actually his own and that he used it for target practice. Jackson said that, if needed, he would present some minitargets he also owned that he used to practice with. The judge then set Liko Kenney's bail at $10,000 cash with probation supervision.

Liko Kenney later pleaded guilty to the charges of assaulting a police officer and resisting arrest for the January 26 standoff with Bruce McKay in Fox Hill Park. He was sentenced to twelve months in jail but would only serve fifteen days behind bars. Kenney was ordered by Judge Jean K. Burling to be "on good behavior" and have "no direct or indirect contact with Bruce McKay." Grafton County attorney Rick St. Hilaire claimed later that Bruce McKay had actually worked behind the scenes to help Liko Kenney get a lighter sentence. In a statement released shortly after the deadly confrontation in May 2007, St. Hilaire wrote of the 2003 incident, "The offenses could have resulted in a sentence of prison time. However, Officer Bruce McKay expressed his desire that compassion be shown to the defendant. He [McKay] supported a short 15-day term of incarceration in the county jail, which was accepted by the court."

Liko Kenney's transformation from unbridled rebel to cold-blooded killer began slowly during the winter of 2007. While his parents were enjoying the warmth and beauty of their coffee farm in Hawaii, Liko took up the personal challenge of surviving the harsh weather alone for the first time in his parents' cabin on the grounds of the Tamarack Tennis Camp. Liko had always voiced his fear and suspicion of those in law enforcement, so no doubt he surprised even himself when he picked up the phone and dialed New Hampshire State Trooper Bret Beausoleil just after 7 P.M. on January 8, 2007, to report that his .45 caliber Hi-Point (the gun he later used to kill Bruce McKay) had been stolen from his cabin the day before, along with a pornographic DVD. Liko told Beausoleil that he believed a young cousin had taken the items. Liko claimed the fifteen-year-old boy had also stolen his Sony Play-

Station (which he had purchased from a pawnshop in Oregon) in the summer of 2006. Liko told the trooper that he eventually got the video game back but that the teenager was no longer allowed into his home. Liko also said that he had spoken with the boy, who denied the theft.

"Why did you wait a day to report the crime?" Beausoleil asked.

"I wanted to give him a chance to return it," Liko replied.

"Where was the handgun stored?"

"It was in my bedroom underneath the mattress," Liko told him. "He [the fifteen-year-old] didn't know where it was." Liko said he first believed the cousin had attempted to steal the PlayStation power cord because he had found it rolled up when he got home. "He's the only one I know who winds up power cords," Liko told the trooper. "I didn't know that he had taken the gun instead." Liko also said that along with the rolled-up power cord, he had discovered a pair of muddy footprints that appeared to be from skateboard shoes a couple sizes smaller than his own. Liko also noticed that a 30/30 rifle had been moved from its position in his bedroom and that the cousin had expressed an interest in it before. Liko didn't think the boy had ever handled a gun before and he was concerned the boy would give the gun to a friend or that it could eventually end up in a school.

Trooper Beausoleil interviewed the boy at Woody and Holly Miller's home a few days later. The boy claimed that Liko burst into his bedroom, questioned him about the theft, and choked him. "I'll break your legs if police don't get to the bottom of the matter," Liko allegedly told the teen. The fifteen-year-old then admitted that he and a friend had gone to Liko's house to steal the power cord and that he had rolled it up. "I didn't take it because it wasn't the right one," the boy said. He said his friend had taken the handgun from Liko's bedroom. When Trooper Beausoleil questioned the friend about his role in the matter, the boy came clean. "The truth is, I took the gun," he admitted. The friend said that he had been sitting on Liko's bed when he felt the gun under the pillow. The boy pulled the weapon out from under the pillow and held it in his hands before quickly returning it. After a second thought, he retrieved the gun once more and decided to take it home. When Beausoleil asked the friend why he had taken the gun, the boy said he was angry at his mother. "She said I was old enough to have a gun and promised to get me a rifle."

On January 16, 2007, Liko Kenney called Bret Beausoleil at the Troop F barracks and told him that he had gotten his gun back. Liko then demanded that his fifteen-year-old cousin and his friend both be charged with stealing the firearm. At this point, Trooper Beausoleil asked Liko if he had confronted his young family member about the theft. "I shook him up a bit," Liko admitted. "And told him he'd better get the gun back or he was going to get hurt." The investigator also later found out that Liko had taken some of the boy's belongings as retaliation and that he had been so concerned the relative would try to turn the tables on him he had offered his own plea deal. "You don't charge me with simple assault," Liko told the boy. "And I won't press charges against you." Beausoleil called Kenney and read him the riot act. "You shouldn't be calling the cops to solve a crime you are the victim of and then go out and commit your own series of offenses!" The trooper then informed Liko that he would be charged with assault and that he could also be charged with witness tampering for trying to negotiate with the fifteen-year-old. Liko Kenney had placed his confidence with police only to find himself charged with a crime as a result. Of course, Liko's infamous temper was responsible for his current predicament. Still, he felt that he was the real victim in this case and that law enforcement was once again treating him like a criminal.

Liko was arraigned on a charge of simple assault in March 2007, yet he was confident the case would not move forward and shared his prediction with Bret Beausoleil. What the trooper did not know was that Liko had placed a phone call to other relatives of the boy, warning that "bad things would happen if they [the boy and his grandmother] showed up for court." Liko also allegedly told the relatives that if he had to go to jail for simple assault, he would kill the witnesses once he got out. Once Trooper Beausoleil learned of the threats, he offered to arrest Liko on the spot and without a warrant. The boy and his grandmother declined the offer because of outside pressure from other members of the Kenney clan, who believed Liko was the least to blame for the whole mess. The fifteen-year-old and his grandmother did testify against Liko at his trial, which took place on April 24, 2007 (roughly two weeks before the fatal shooting). Liko represented himself at trial and told the judge that he did in fact assault the teen, but that he did it out of fear for his own safety. Liko believed the boy was hiding the gun in his pocket and was getting ready to use it against him. Liko could not sway the judge and was found guilty and ordered to pay a $250 fine.

After leaving the court room, Liko walked down the stairs to the clerk's office where he asked one of his uncles to pay the fine. Beausoleil confronted Liko and told him that he knew about the threatening phone call. "I'm just a phone call away from charging you with witness tampering," the trooper said.

"Is that a threat?" Kenney asked.

"I'm just letting you know what I could do," Beausoleil responded. The trooper explained that the only reason he hadn't charged Liko with witness tampering was because the witnesses did not want him charged. Liko left the courthouse without paying the $250 fine.

Intimidation was as much a part of Liko Kenney's makeup as it was of Bruce McKay's. A few weeks before his trial for simple assault, Liko put a scare into his former principal at Profile High School, Richard Larcom, while he and his wife Donna were getting ready for a late-afternoon stroll with their three dogs up Paine Road in Franconia. The couple was kneeling at the end of their driveway when they suddenly heard the roar of a speeding car coming their way. The Larcoms looked up and saw that the vehicle was now on the shoulder of the road and headed straight toward them as it sprayed a torrent of water up from a shallow burrow pit between the road and a snowbank. All the while, Liko Kenney was leaned over into the passenger side of his Toyota Celica with the middle finger of his right hand pressed firmly against the windshield. The Larcoms grabbed their three dogs and held them tightly against the snowbank. They had nowhere to run and Kenney had the gas pedal pressed down to the floor. Richard and Donna Larcom closed their eyes as the maverick machine drew closer. At the last second, Liko jerked the wheel away from the spot where the Larcoms were standing. The couple felt a whoosh of air pass by as they both held their breath. When the Larcoms finally opened their eyes, they saw a pair of deep tire tracks in the snow and mud just about one foot from where they were standing. The couple did not recognize exactly who the driver was until the Toyota Celica pulled away. That's when the Larcoms realized they had just crossed paths with Liko Kenney. The couple also realized that their brief moment of terror was not over. Paine Road was a dead-end street in the winter and that meant Liko Kenney would have to turn around and pass them again to get back to the main road. Richard Larcom also believed that this wasn't some spur-of-the-moment prank on Liko Kenney's part. The high school principal and his wife shared the road with just a few other residents and he knew that none of them were friendly with the young man. *No, he's come down here for me,* Larcom thought to himself. The couple didn't want to wait for Liko to turn around and head back their way, so they immediately retreated back to their home with their three dogs in tow. Before they got halfway up the driveway, the Toyota Celica came into view once again. Liko Kenney was speeding down the road on the wrong side, the side closest to the Larcoms' driveway. He had the window down and once again he was flipping the couple off with his middle finger. As Liko approached the foot of the driveway, he slowed down. "Fuck you, you worthless piece of shit!" he screamed before speeding off again.

Liko Kenney was a tightly wound spool of passion and fury and he was beginning to unravel at a frightening pace. It could have been the stress surrounding his latest court case, or it could have been the pressure of living alone for the first time at Tamarack. It is possible that cabin fever had finally caught up with the young man. Liko was engaged in a constant inner struggle between both sides of himself. On the one hand, he was a "gentle hippie" who had recently adopted four-day-old chicks and was raising them on his parents' property, but, as family members say, there had always been some darkness in his soul and that darkness was now taking over Liko Kenney's fragile mind. Shortly after the deadly showdown on Route 116, Bill Kenney walked through his nephew's cabin, looking for any sign of Liko's descent into madness. He found a disturbing clue in the young man's journal. On the last page, Liko Kenney had scribbled *MY LAST DAYS.*

As a long-haired, wide-eyed child, Liko Kenney with his family spent half the year living on the grounds of the Tamarack Tennis Camp and the other half at their coffee farm in Hawaii.
(Courtesy Michele Kenney)

A celebratory Liko Kenney with his fist raised high in the air. This image is now seen on posters and bumper stickers across the North Country.
(Courtesy Michele Kenney)

Bruce McKay celebrating his graduation from high school with his sister Meggen and his mother Catherine.
(Courtesy Meggen McKay-Payerle)

Franconia Police Corporal N. Bruce McKay. The officer issued a warning to his comrades about Liko Kenney shortly before he was killed.
(Courtesy Meggen McKay-Payerle)

Screen grab from Officer McKay's patrol camera showing McKay macing Liko Kenney.

Screen grab from Officer McKay's patrol camera showing Kenney shooting McKay in the back.

A shirtless Greg Floyd and son being questioned by police at the
crime scene. Authorities have painted Floyd as a reluctant hero but critics
argue that he should have been investigated for his role in the tragedy.

The .45 caliber Hi-Point semi-automatic pistol Liko Kenney used to kill
Corporal Bruce McKay. The weapon had had several previous owners and
all had complained about its lack of reliability.

(Courtesy New Hampshire State Police)

The .45 caliber Sig Sauer pistol issued to Officer McKay and later used
by Gregory Floyd to kill Liko Kenney.

(Courtesy New Hampshire State Police)

Witness Caleb Macaulay photographed by investigators after the tragedy. Macaulay was one of many townspeople familiar with the long-standing feud between Liko Kenney and Bruce McKay.
(Courtesy New Hampshire State Police)

Liko Kenney's Toyota Celica photographed after it had been lifted off the body of Bruce McKay. The impact of the collision had crushed McKay's pelvis and torn off part of his nose.
(Courtesy New Hampshire State Police)

Bruce McKay's police cruiser parked at the crime scene. The vehicle's video camera had captured the chase and fatal stop of Liko Kenney.

Sugar Hill Police Sergeant David Wentworth was the first to investigate the crime scene; he voiced his concerns about the moving of evidence.

Bill Kenney's home. It is just one of many rustic cabins built along 460 acres of the Tamarack Tennis Camp.
(Photo by author)

The Franconia Village Store shows its pride for hometown hero Bode Miller on the outside; on the inside, much of the talk revolves around Miller's cousin Liko Kenney.
(Photo by author)

Bill Kenney standing next to his nephew Liko's grave. The tombstone reads "Me Ke Aloha Pau'ole" or "With never-ending love."

(Photo by author)

Greg Floyd enters the courtroom for his April 15, 2008, trial on
criminal threatening charges. Floyd was found guilty and later exploded
outside the courtroom.

(Photo by author)

Liko Kenney's Toyota Celica in storage in Franconia, New Hampshire. The author was taken here by Chris King and Brad Whipple—two men who refuse to let this case die.

(Photo by author)

This exclusive photograph shows the view into the driver's-side window of the Toyota Celica. Liko Kenney's dried blood is caked on the seat cushion and seat belt.

(Photo by author)

There is no grief like
the grief that does not speak.
HENRY WADSWORTH LONGFELLOW

May 11, 2007

Sharon Davis drove with great speed up Route 93 North toward Littleton Hospital, her fears worsening every second. Fortunately, Sharon knew exactly where she was headed; in fact, she and Bruce had visited the hospital together once before. With their wedding just a few short months away, Sharon was looking for a job closer to the home they were sharing in Landaff. She had once stopped by the Littleton Hospital to check out the job board and see if there was an opening for a veteran microbiologist.

She pulled into the hospital parking lot and felt her heart pounding. She then walked on weak knees toward the emergency room. *Oh my God, what's happened? Is he alive? Is he dead?* At this point she had no idea and was unsure whether she actually wanted to find out. She entered the ER and was surprised to find the waiting room completely deserted. Suddenly Bruce's former wife Angela came out of a room with daughter Courtney. Angela looked Sharon in the eye and, although they had had their differences in the past, at this moment they were one.

"Bruce has . . ." Angela's lowered lip trembled as she struggled to find the words. "Bruce has passed away."

Sharon let out an agonizing scream and ran out of the hospital in tears. Sergeant David Wentworth, Bruce's longtime friend, followed her.

"Who did this?" Sharon asked angrily.

Wentworth shook his head. "I can't tell you. It's still under investigation."

"I know who did this!" Sharon screamed. Her thoughts immediately took her back to that terrifying encounter at the Littleton Wal-Mart. "It's a local guy with long hair." She knew his face but for the life of her could not remember his name: "It's Bode Miller's cousin!"

Wentworth said nothing. Instead he shook his head again. Sharon struggled to regain her composure as she returned to the emergency room and hugged young Courtney, who was crying softly for her daddy. After a few heart-wrenching moments with her fiancée's daughter, Sharon finally asked to see Bruce. She was led into a room and offered a chair next to Bruce's bed. "When I first saw him, his head was completely covered in dressing," she remembers. "He had a deep wound between his eyes and nose. I thought he'd been executed." His broken body was covered with a blanket from the neck down and she had no idea of the massive trauma to his torso and legs. Sharon instinctively reached for Bruce's hand. It was still warm. "Sorry, but you can't do that," said a police officer in attendance. "The body is evidence." Instead, Sharon was allowed to hold one of Bruce's fingers. She stayed in that room for what seemed like an eternity as she remembered what once was and thought about what never could be.

✤ The time was 9:25 P.M., May 11, 2007, and Caleb Macaulay was shaken, but ready to tell investigators what had happened just three hours before on Route 116/Easton Road in Franconia. He was sitting in the interview room at New Hampshire State Police Troop F in Twin Mountain, nestled between Franconia Notch and Crawford Notch. The air was stifling and Macaulay's wrists were still sore from the handcuffs he had been wearing and his eyes still held the faint sting of the pepper spray he had been doused with while sitting in the passenger seat of Liko Kenney's Toyota Celica. The spray had also given him a burning sensation on both arms. He had been treated by EMTs three times but the pain kept coming back. Sergeant Michael Marshall of the state police read the

Miranda rights to Macaulay, who said he understood every word. Marshall then asked Caleb for permission to record his statement. Macaulay gave his consent and Marshall pressed the record button on the tape recorder.

As the trooper was getting the basic questions out of the way; name, age, date of birth, he also conducted a search of the young man's hands with a gunshot evidence residue kit. Caleb held his hands out in front of the officer and then turned them over. Sergeant Marshall asked him about a cut on his left hand under his thumb. Macaulay explained that the injury happened while he was working as a dishwasher at Cannon Mountain a few months prior. Someone had left a knife in the sink and Caleb had accidently run his hand over it. There were a few other scratches to his hands, which he blamed on his mother's cat. Satisfied with the explanations, the trooper rubbed the residue kit over Caleb's fingers, scratching his skin like sandpaper.

"When was the last time that you did fire a firearm?" Sergeant Marshall asked. A nervous Macaulay told the investigator that he enjoyed target shooting occasionally but that, unlike many of his friends, he was not a real gun enthusiast. "I have a compact bow."

"Did you handle a firearm at all today?" the trooper asked.

"I did not," Macaulay replied. "The guy who picked up Officer McKay's gun and shot the driver, I ducked, but he picked up the gun, I'm like, sir, I'm not gonna pick up that gun, you're gonna shoot me if I pick up the gun so I didn't touch any weapon whatsoever."

"He told you to pick up what gun?"

"He told me to pick up my friend's .45 out of his dead hands," Caleb replied. "I was scared for my life 'cause he had the gun nonstop pointing at me. . . . I mean I understand what he did, he stood up for a cop and he was doing a great job. I didn't know who he was and he sounded really crazy at the time so I was like really scared." The events of the past few hours were flashing nonstop through Macaulay's mind. The young man could hardly believe that he had actually survived the ordeal. He could still feel the air from the bullet as it flew past him into his friend.

So far during the interview, the key material witness in this case was all over the map in his statement, going from subject to subject without any clear linear thought. The trooper knew this was quite understandable considering what Caleb Macaulay had just gone through. It was Sergeant Mike Marshall's job to slow down the pace and force Caleb to concentrate. Marshall continued to methodically examine the young man's hands for gunpowder residue while Macaulay talked about anything that entered his mind. "I thank you guys for making this very easy for the whole situation that's going on right now, I know you don't know me from a hole in the wall but like I said, I just want to get home and see my family and friends and stay quiet for awhile. . . . I don't want to talk; I don't want to do anything."

While Caleb Macaulay was having his hands examined in the interview room of the Troop F State Police barracks, Greg Floyd was just sitting down with investigators in the Detectives Office downstairs. His interview was conducted by Sergeant Charles West of the state police. First, West attempted to calm Floyd's nerves by telling him that he was not under arrest and that he could leave at any time. Still, he had Floyd sign a Miranda form and tried to explain to the man his rights. West told Floyd that he had a right to remain silent and that anything he said could be used against him in a court of law. The ex-Marine did not like the sound of this. "I don't think I need a lawyer, I have . . . I don't think I've done anything wrong," Floyd insisted. "I don't think you're gonna charge me with murder or anything because basically I was defending someone that was helpless." Floyd went on to explain what he had been doing in Franconia and why he was headed south on Route 116/Easton Road in the late afternoon. He told the trooper that he and his son Gregory had seen Corporal Bruce McKay ram Liko Kenney's Toyota Celica with his police cruiser.

"Is that right? Now were you still moving when you see the car being pushed up?" Trooper West asked. "What are you doing?" Floyd said that he heard a gunshot and then pulled his son down and away from the windshield. Floyd peeked over the dashboard and saw McKay running across the road as blood gushed from a wound on his side. "And they [Liko Kenney and Caleb Macaulay] come behind him in a car and run him over, okay, and they back up and, you know, hit him again and the gun comes flying out the window. Now I believe the gun was still the perpetrator's, I'm not positive. [It was later determined that the weapon fell out of Corporal McKay's hand.] . . . I picked it up and leaned in to see what this guy [Liko] was doing and, you know, pressed my elbow into the passenger's throat to hold him in place and the other guy was trying to jack a round into the ten millimeter . . . he's trying with both hands to unjam his gun, because for some reason he'd get one bullet in the chamber but the second bullet behind it wouldn't let the slide shut, but anyway while he was doing that, I just, I just shot him. . . . I didn't give him much time, maybe twice of this [*he demonstrates Kenney's attempt to jack a round*] and I shot him."

"All right, did you say anything to [Liko] before you fired?" West asked.

"No I didn't."

🖐 Upstairs in the interview room, New Hampshire State Police Sergeant Michael Marshall was trying to gauge just how fast Liko Kenney was driving when Corporal McKay pulled him over. What neither Marshall nor Macaulay knew was the fact that McKay had pulled Liko over for an expired registration, not a speeding infraction. "He [Liko] likes to play around," Macaulay told the trooper. "He has a car that's sort of like fun and I told him, I'm like, 'Liko'—he's already had issues with cops—I'm like, 'Liko, we were gonna go to Oregon . . . let's just chill out.' He likes to drive fast and I didn't even think he was going 47 mph. I think he was only going 45 mph, I thought, 'cause he slowed down right to 35 mph within a second and that's why I was like, 'Why are the [police] lights coming on?' And then when McKay went to pull him over, that I was sort of questioning it. I was like, 'What's going on?' I was sort of weirded out." Macaulay told West that McKay never told Liko Kenney the reason he had stopped him. He then described how Liko tensed up once he realized that McKay was behind the wheel of the police cruiser. "He rolled down the window just a crack so he could talk to the officer, but I mean I've never really seen Liko really scared like that before. I mean, I know I'm not like gonna bring up the past history, but I know he said he had issues; they both had issues with each other. . . . It's like the little vendetta thing they play on each other."

"I guess we've established that you feel there was bad blood between them," Sergeant Marshall pointed out. Macaulay explained that Liko had attempted to call his uncle at the Tamarack Tennis Camp, and over the next several minutes, he gave Sergeant Marshall the Cliff's Notes version of the Kenney family history there. Caleb then described to Trooper Marshall what happened after Liko backed his Celica into the dirt parking area in front of Joel McKenzie's garage. "The keys weren't out of the ignition but we were stopped. We were actually taking off our seat belts, and that's when I heard, I just started hearing Liko yell, "You rammed my car! Stop, stop, stop!" And he [McKay] just kept like driving. First he [McKay] bumped it, like I thought he was just bumping it at first, and then he just took it all the way, rammed it all the way so we were like stuck." Caleb then watched as McKay jumped out of the cruiser with a canister of pepper spray in his hand and doused them both. "And then all I heard was gunshots and it wasn't, I'm pretty sure it wasn't directed at our car, it was shooting *out* of our car, which was Liko's .45."

"Did Liko fire first?" Sergeant Marshall asked. Caleb Macaulay said he couldn't see much due to the amount of pepper spray in his eyes but that he believed so, because if McKay had fired first, there would have been shattering glass in the car or either Liko or himself would have been hit. "Okay, where did Liko get the gun from?" Marshall asked. "I mean right then and there, where did, where did he retrieve it? From his waistband? From a jacket?"

"I'm pretty sure it was on the floor," Caleb replied, although not completely confident of his answer. "I don't know. I don't think it was tucked under the seat, I think it was just on the floor under, by his seat." Caleb told the investigator that he knew Liko kept a gun in his car but did not know it was loaded. "He [Liko] always told me that it wasn't loaded."

❦ As Caleb Macaulay continued to describe the shooting of Corporal Bruce McKay, Greg Floyd remained downstairs in the Detectives Office where he and State Police Sergeant Charles West were going over his role in this bloody drama.

"Where did you hit him [Liko]?" West asked Floyd.

"I believe right here," Floyd replied, pointing to his right shoulder. "You know, I mean, I could have put two in his, directly in his heart, but I wasn't thinking about killing nobody, but I'm not going to sit there and watch an innocent man being run over time and again, time and again." Floyd said he was convinced that Kenney was trying to kill Bruce McKay.

"You had said earlier that you've seen people shot before."

"Yah," Floyd replied, nodding his head.

"What's your background?"

"I was in the Marine Corps," Floyd said proudly.

"Vietnam era?"

Floyd nodded his head once more. "Uh, yah, Vietnam era. I was in the Special Forces of the Marine Corps and then I worked for the government in places and things you can't talk about."

Sergeant West was confused by Floyd's bold statement. "So were you in, were you in Vietnam?" he pressed.

"Uh, not in that way," the ex-Marine tried to explain. "I worked on special projects. . . . I wasn't a grunt."

Sergeant West then asked Floyd if he had a criminal record.

"Yes, I do," he replied matter-of-factly.

"And what is it for?"

Greg Floyd paused for a moment. "Uh, pot."

"So you're a convicted felon?"

"Right," Floyd answered. West continued this line of questioning and asked Floyd if he'd ever been charged with a more serious crime. "Uh, yah, they called it PCP, but we called it THC," Floyd answered. "It was back when the stuff was just getting started; you know what I mean. . . . And I just got out of the service and I'm running around being Johnny Stud or trying to. But I made a mistake, plain and simple."

The interview then steered back to the moment Liko Kenney struck Bruce McKay with his car. "Somehow or another, that tough sonofabitch got up," Floyd recalled in amazement. "I mean that's pure torture. You know, if you're gonna kill somebody, be man enough to knock on their door and tell 'em to go get their own pistol. . . . You know somebody said they have a history, the officer and the guy. . . . Well I'm thinking, I'm worried because you know I'm a felon and I've taken a risk, but I'm not gonna allow a man to be killed by being run over. . . . I'm just not made that way." Greg Floyd then proceeded to clarify or contradict his earlier statement concerning the shooting of Liko Kenney. "I'm all set and ready to shoot and I'm screaming either 'put it down' or 'you're gonna die.'"

"Yah, well, I asked you that before," Sergeant West pointed out. "Was there any conversation? What were you saying?"

"I'm saying, 'put it down; leave it alone. You know you wanna live.' Whatever come into my mind that I thought he might let it go."

While Floyd was changing his story, Caleb Macaulay described the event much differently during his interview with State Trooper Michael Marshall.

"What did that man [Floyd] say?" Marshall asked. "As he walked up, what did he say? You've [already] driven up, the car's on top of McKay."

"He started shooting," Macaulay replied.

"He did? Did he say anything?"

"He said nothing, he started shooting," Caleb reiterated. "And then he had both guns pointed at me . . . he acted like a cop, but like I said, he went off on a sort of crazy spell . . . he just kept going off. I'm like, 'Sir, can you stop talking about what you just did?' Like, I was really traumatized and he kept [saying], 'Oh I shot him good,' and stuff like that. I did not want to hear any of that."

As the interview neared its conclusion, Macaulay asked where the case was headed. Marshall told him that they hadn't reached any conclusions yet. "Can you guys sorta step by step let me know what going on?" Caleb pleaded. "'Cause I'm sorta scared, like I've never been in. I feel like I'm in such a deep hole right now. . . . It's a real nightmare."

⚜ The nightmare was just beginning for the families of both Liko Kenney and Corporal Bruce McKay. Several attempts to revive the officer were unsuccessful and Bruce McKay was declared dead soon after the ambulance arrived at Littleton Regional Hospital. Autopsies were performed on both men the following day, May 12, 2007. In the examination of Corporal Bruce McKay, New Hampshire's Chief Medical Examiner Dr. Thomas A. Andrew noted the following: five wounds caused by a firearm: a superficial through and through injury to the right forearm, and four wounds to the right side. Corporal McKay also had blunt-impact injuries, including lacerations to the scalp, a laceration to the nose and lower lip, a fracture to the skull, a laceration to the upper left groin region, a fracture to the left pelvis, and a laceration below the left knee. Four projectiles were recovered from Corporal McKay's body during the autopsy. The cause of death was multiple gunshot wounds. The manner of death was homicide. Toxicology testing revealed an incidental finding of caffeine. Forensic testing later revealed that the four discharged bullets recovered from Bruce McKay's body during autopsy matched Liko Kenney's pistol.

When Dr. Andrew performed the autopsy on Liko Kenney's body he noted two wounds caused by a firearm, one to the right side of the head and a through and through wound with an entry to the right side of the neck and the exit on the left. Liko also had a faint, oily orange residue on the right side of his face (consistent with OC spray). The cause of death was two gunshot wounds, one to the head and one to the neck. The manner of death was homicide. Toxicology testing revealed the presence of THC, which indicated recent consumption of marijuana prior to death. There were also incidental findings of caffeine and theobromine (likely a metabolite of caffeine or chocolate). Forensic testing later revealed that one discharged bullet and fragments recovered from Liko's body during autopsy matched Corporal McKay's gun.

The Major Crime Unit of the New Hampshire State Police also conducted a thorough sweep of the crime scene itself. Some of that evidence was later taken to the New Hampshire State Police Forensic Laboratory in Concord. In their report, crime scene investigators noted a blood trail on Route 116 that extended across to the opposite side of the road. They also retrieved two handguns with spent shell casings. One firearm had belonged to Corporal Bruce McKay. The .45 caliber Sig Sauer semi-automatic pistol had one live Federal round in the chamber and a magazine with one live Federal round. The other firearm, a .45 caliber Hi-Point semi-automatic pistol belonging to Liko Kenney, had one live Winchester round in it and a magazine with three live Winchester rounds. Five spent Winchester .45 caliber shell casings were found on the ground near the front of the police cruiser. Two others were discovered between the hood and windshield of Liko Kenney's Toyota Celica. Six spent Federal .45 caliber shell casings were found on the grass near Liko's car. One live Winchester .45 caliber round was found near the same spot along with a .45 caliber bullet. Another bullet was discovered inside a red barn on Joel and Connie McKenzie's property. The projectile had entered the barn on the side and was found in a toolbox. A discharged bullet jacket was also recovered at the scene.

Chapter 159 of the New Hampshire state gun law states that only a city mayor, town selectman, chief of police, or full-time police officer can grant a permit for a person to carry a loaded pistol or revolver; the applicant must indicate (1) good reason to fear injury to the applicant's person or property; or (2) any other proper purpose, such as hunting, target shooting, or self-defense. Liko Kenney may have had good reason to fear injury, but of course he had never sought a permit to carry his gun. The trail of ownership of the .45 caliber Hi-Point semi-automatic begins in April 2003, when a man by the name of Scott John Walker bought the firearm at the Village Gun Store in Whitefield, New Hampshire. Walker told investigators that he purchased the pistol to carry with him while bear hunting. Walker worked as a cook at the Dairy Bar restaurant in Franconia at the time. He said he had never liked the pistol, calling it "cheap" and "a piece of junk" because it frequently jammed. Walker had only had it for a few months before he sold it to Steve Dunleavey, a coworker at the Dairy Bar. Dunleavey had seen the weapon in Walker's truck and had expressed an interest in buying it from him. Walker sold the pistol to Dunleavey in July 2003 after typing up a bill of sale that both men had signed. Along with the gun, the deal also included two clips and fifty rounds of ammunition. When police tracked Dunleavey down approximately one month after the McKay shooting, the man could barely remember the transaction. He did recollect that he paid $150 for it but no longer had the bill of sale. Dunleavey claimed he had only shot the gun once and that it jammed on every fifth round. He said he sold the gun to "some guy" in Franconia, but couldn't remember who. "Maybe my ex-girlfriend knows," he told investigators. "Why don't you go ask her?"

When police approached Brenda Saunders at her trailer home

that same day, she told them she had been with Steven Dunleavey for twenty years and that she knew the weapon they were talking about. The purchase of the firearm had been a point of contention with the couple. Saunders had gone to the extreme of hiding it on him because she did not trust him with it.

"So who did Dunleavey sell the gun to?" the officer asked. Saunders was unsure at first until the phone inside her trailer rang. Another woman inside the trailer answered the phone and then shouted, "Matt Chernicki!" The officers figured the person on the phone was Steve Dunleavey. Brenda Saunders reiterated that her former boyfriend had in fact sold the gun to Matthew Chernicki. Chernicki was a close friend of Liko Kenney; when he finally met with investigators at the Easton Fire Department, Chernicki told them that he was "mentally unbalanced" and upset after burying his friend. When asked about the gun, Chernicki said he'd had it in his possession for only eight months. He claimed he then sold it to the Kenneys; when pressed, however, he admitted that he had sold it directly to Liko. "Liko hated McKay," he told the officers. He said his friend would get angry at the mere sight of a Franconia police cruiser. "I thought Liko killed McKay with a Colt?" The officers explained that Bruce McKay had been shot with Liko Kenney's .45 caliber Hi-Point.

At the crime scene, investigators also found Bruce McKay's sunglasses, a police radio, and an OC container on the McKenzies' front lawn. There was also a deep blood stain in the grassy area where McKay had been trapped under Kenney's car. Inside the Toyota Celica, the first thing they noticed was the driver himself. Liko Kenney was wearing a T-shirt and shorts and was seated in the driver's seat with his hands on his lap. Investigators noted blood on the inside of the car and blood spatter on Kenney's body. The driver's-side window was down most of the way and the sunroof was partially open. The window on the passenger side was fully up but the glass was in fragments. Broken glass was found inside and outside the car. The windshield was cracked and had a bullet hole in the lower cowling. There was damage to the front of the car caused by McKay's SUV and by Liko Kenney himself when he struck the officer. The spoiler under the vehicle's front bumper was cracked and had a blood smear near the crack. The following items were also recovered from Liko Kenney's car.

- A metal smoking pipe
- Juice and a half-gallon of vodka
- A lead projectile fragment from the front windshield
- A Nokia Trac Fone on top of the center console (The Trac Fone was examined and found to contain a record of several outgoing calls. Three calls were placed to three different phone numbers around the time of the incident. According to the Trac Fone's records, the calls were placed at 6:05 P.M., 6:06 P.M., and 6:07 P.M.
- A film canister containing what appeared to be marijuana seeds
- A piece of cloth and a rag were also found on the driver's-side floor
- An empty handgun magazine on the driver's-side floor underneath Kenney's right leg.
- Two bags containing water with one bag containing one goldfish; the other bag containing four goldfish. All fish were dead.

Bruce McKay's SUV was still in good shape. The only damage could be found on the cruiser's front license plate, which was bent. Inside the vehicle, investigators retrieved the cruiser video and a radar readout that was locked with a target speed of 54 mph and a patrol speed of 39 mph. There were also deep tire impressions in the dirt both in front of and behind the cruiser.

Inside the vehicle investigators recovered the following items.

- Mossberg 12-gauge pump shotgun containing eight rounds with none in the chamber

- Coltar 15 A-2 assault rifle, .223 caliber, with a full magazine and no rounds in the chamber
- Black nylon ammo case with three full magazines with .223 caliber rounds
- OC training card
- Patrolman's hat with badge
- Map of the White Mountains
- Tactical Baton certification card
- Fraternal Order of Police membership card

Several more items were taken directly from Corporal McKay's body, including his police badge, an empty OC spray holder, twenty-seven cents in change, and a medallion he had worn on a chain around his neck. The medallion paid tribute to Saint Michael, believed to be the patron saint of police officers. The pendant was designed to show Michael the Archangel with his wings spread and his pointed spear running through the neck of a serpent. The inscription read simply SAINT MICHAEL PROTECT US.

And there was a great battle in heaven, Michael and his angels
fought with the dragon, and the dragon and his angels fought back.
But he was not strong enough, and they lost their place in heaven.

REVELATION 12:7–8

In the coming days, the national media descended on the tiny community of Franconia Notch and many newspapers, including the *New York Times*, put their own spin on the shooting. In an article that ran under the headline "Deaths of Skier's Cousin and Officer Divide Town," reporter Nathaniel Vinton called it, "the bloody culmination of a bitter long-running feud that seemingly everyone in this small town knew about but no one was able to stop." Vinton's description of McKay and Liko Kenney's shared history was spot-on although his reporting of the actual story had one major flaw. Vinton wrote that Liko had an agreement with Franconia police that allowed for an additional officer to be present if and when he was stopped by Bruce McKay. Vinton attributed this information to "several residents." The reality was that there was no special agreement between Liko and law enforcement. A brief look at the small size of the Franconia Police Department (three officers and the chief) should have signaled to any reporter that such an accommodation would be virtually impossible. On May 12, 2007, one day after the tragedy, the *Union Leader* ran the headline "Police Officer Fatally Shot."

New Hampshire Attorney General Kelly Ayotte told reporters that the victim was a Franconia police officer but she refused to release his name pending notification of his relatives. Bruce McKay's family stretched from New Hampshire down to Charlotte, North Carolina, where his mother Catherine now resided. Ayotte also would not confirm the identity of the officer's killer. Word that Liko Kenney was involved came from his uncle Bill Kenney, who told the *Union Leader*, "We lost one of the sons of the valley here. He was born right here, part of the Kenney family. He's famous or infamous; however you want to look at it. One of the clan." The comment by Liko's uncle, which focused attention and a touch of sympathy toward the killer in this case, allowed for the great divide between the government and the people that would continue to build as this drama played out. Officials did their best to keep the focus primarily on the fallen officer. New Hampshire Governor John Lynch, a Democrat, then serving his second term, was quick to release a statement on the night of the killings: "The murder of a police officer strikes at the very heart of our society, and the loss of this police officer will be felt by all the people of New Hampshire. We honor this officer's courage, service, and commitment and extend our deepest sympathies to this officer's family, friends, community, and brothers and sisters in law enforcement." These were not just hollow words from the state's chief executive officer. Lynch had gone down this road all too recently; another of New Hampshire's "finest" had been gunned down in the line of duty just seven months before.

❧ Thirty-five-year-old Michael Briggs was known for having a big smile to match his large build. He wore two uniforms around the city of Manchester, New Hampshire; one blue and the other yellow to match his son's Little League team, which he coached. It was 2:45 A.M. on the chilly morning of October 16, 2006, and Michael Briggs had only fifteen minutes left on his shift. Briggs had always volunteered for extra shifts so that his wife Laura could be a stay-at-home mom. He and his partner, Officer John Breckinridge, had been patrolling one of Manchester's toughest neighborhoods when they got a report of "shots fired" in the vicinity of Lincoln Street, right between Lake Avenue and Central Street. The call had come in as some kind of "domestic incident," allegedly involving twenty-six-year-old Michael "Styx" Addison, a man well known to police in both New Hampshire and Massachusetts.

Addison, a father of three illegitimate children, had been one of the first juveniles to be prosecuted as an adult under Massachusetts Youthful Offender law when, at the age of sixteen, he pointed a loaded revolver at another teen's face and pulled the trigger twice. There were two bullets in the gun but the weapon jammed and did not fire. Addison was arrested again a year later and charged with knifing and robbing a member of his own basketball team. He served three years behind bars shuttling between juvenile detention centers and state prison.

Once released from custody, Addison continued on a violent path but he was New Hampshire's problem to deal with now. He had moved north from the crime-infested streets of Boston's poorest neighborhoods to Manchester, New Hampshire, which faced a growing criminal element of its own. He had been recently charged with robbing a 7-Eleven in Hudson and a shooting on Edward J. Roy Drive in Manchester, where bullets missed a father and his son by just a few inches. He had also told friends recently that he would shoot a police officer if one tried to stop him. Now in the predawn hours of October 16, Addison would graduate from a career as a violent, but petty thief to cold-blooded killer. When Officer Briggs approached him and another man near the scene of the crime, Addison was not interested in talking. Instead he raised his gun and fired a single shot through Briggs's bicycle helmet and into his head. The officer, a father of two who a year before had been honored for rushing into a burning building to rescue residents, collapsed to the ground. Briggs's gun never left its holster. The gunman took off immediately sparking a two-state manhunt before finally being captured fifteen hours later while hiding at his grandmother's house in Dorchester, Massachusetts. Michael Briggs was taken to nearby Elliot Hospital where he died the next day.

Two years later, in 2008, Michael Addison stood trial for the murder. Lawyers for Addison did not deny their client had shot Briggs; they did claim, however, the shooting was not an intentional act and therefore Addison should be convicted of second-degree murder. Prosecutors called it "a conscious and deadly choice to pull the trigger and end Officer Briggs' life." The jury agreed with the state and Michael "Styx" Addison was found guilty of capital murder. The sentencing phase immediately followed, prompting Briggs's widow Laura to take the stand where she described in gut-wrenching detail how she lost "the only stable man I had in my life." On December 22, 2008, Michael Addison was officially sentenced to death for his crime. Addison's death sentence was the first in New Hampshire since 1959.

Officer Michael Briggs had become the fortieth New Hampshire law enforcement officer killed in the line of duty and the eleventh to be murdered. The first to lay down his life was Strafford County Deputy Sheriff Charles E. Smith on May 1, 1891, in the small town of Barrington. Smith was the eldest of six children and a former shoemaker who had fought with the 18th New Hampshire Regiment during the Civil War. The 18th Regiment had seen its share of carnage during the Siege of Petersburg and later at Fort Stedman, where Smith and his comrades repulsed a major attack by Confederate soldiers. Smith later contracted a severe case of rheumatism after being exposed to "wet ground" at City Point, Virginia, and won a medical discharge on May 20, 1865. After the war he married local teacher Ellen J. Decateur; the couple had one son, Jasper, who died shortly after his second birthday.

Instead of wallowing in sorrow over the death of his only son, Smith threw himself into public service. He had served as selectman, town clerk, and collector of taxes before being appointed deputy sheriff for Strafford County. He helped keep order there for six years until the serenity was broken by the crack of a gunshot in the spring of 1891. Smith had been investigating the theft of a carriage and two beautiful light bay horses worth several hundred dollars from a tavern and boardinghouse owned and operated by Josiah R Calef. The suspect, who gave his name as MacDonald, was a "young, well dressed man" in his midtwenties who had taken up lodging at Calef's, claiming to be a medical examiner for a New

York life insurance company. The horses, owned by the B. J. Kendall Spavin Cure Company, were housed in a stable within earshot of Josiah R. Calef's bedroom window. At midnight on May 1, 1891, Calef's wife was awakened by a loud noise coming from the stable; instead of investigating, however, the woman went back to sleep.

It wasn't until the next morning that her husband discovered the carriage and horses missing from the barn. Calef and his stable boy gave chase immediately but ventured out in the wrong direction. Later, around noontime, two other local men offered to track the thief and eventually spotted the carriage hidden in a barn surrounded by thick woods about a mile from Strafford Ridge. The horse thief's trail was surprisingly easy to follow, thanks to a particular shoe one of the horses had on. The trackers summoned Sheriff Smith, who quickly organized a posse of a dozen men and set out for the area known as Sloper Woods. The thief, who was feeding the horses at the time, saw their approach and fled on foot. Smith and his men went charging after him while dodging wild shots from the thief's revolver. A. W. Lyman, a stove peddler who had been tracking "MacDonald" for much of the day, opened fire with his shotgun striking the thief in the back. The man fell to the ground as Sheriff Smith closed in. "Don't come any closer or I'll shoot," he cried, waving his gun toward the posse. Smith pounced on the suspect, hoping to knock the weapon free and was shot once in the pelvis. Bleeding seriously, Smith still managed enough strength to pin the gunman down while others applied shackles to his wrists. The sheriff then rolled over on the ground, covering his seeping wound with a trembling hand.

Seeing their leader in agony, the angry posse decided to forego the formalities of a criminal trial and voted to lynch the horse thief right there in Sloper Woods. Sheriff Smith protested the mob rule and the posse respected the wishes of their wounded sheriff. Sheriff Smith was carried out of Sloper Woods and taken to his home where he was examined by two local physicians who determined that the bullet had entered through the left hip and passed through the rectum. Both doctors believed the bullet was now lodged somewhere in Smith's right hip although they could not find it. The physicians said the odds of Smith's survival were "about even." Despite great pain, the sheriff was alert through the examination and ordered his men to take the prisoner to the local jail. The thief, who now faced more serious charges, told captors that his real name was Julius H. MacArthur and that he was an insurance agent from Calais, Maine. MacArthur claimed the horses were indeed his and that he swapped for them in Epping, New Hampshire.

After several days, doctors finally managed to extract the bullet from Sheriff Smith's hip. The May 15, 1891, edition of the *Rochester Courier* reported that Smith was resting easier but that doctors feared he was in danger of blood poisoning. That fear was well founded. Sheriff Charles E. Smith slipped into unconsciousness and never awoke. He died at 3 A.M. on May 29, 1891. His funeral was one of the largest New Hampshire had ever seen and was attended by approximately three hundred people, many of whom had traveled from every corner of the state. As for Sheriff Smith's killer, police still couldn't confirm his identity. Upon hearing of Smith's death, the so-called Julius H. MacArthur attempted to take his own life by opening an artery in his left arm with what was described as a "large pin" while awaiting trial at the Strafford County Jail. "MacArthur" recovered from his self-inflicted wound but would never be held accountable for his crime. He eventually escaped by slipping out a window in the women's quarters on the second floor of the jailhouse and was never seen or heard from again.

New Hampshire's most shocking murder involving law enforcement officers came more than a century later on the afternoon of August 19, 1997, in the North Country village of Colebrook, population 2,500 and just ten miles south of the Canadian border. On that day, the face of agitated loner Carl Drega would become forever seared in the minds of New Hampshire's people. On the official town Web site, Colebrook is described in Rockwellian terms: "Located within sight of Dixville Notch in the State's most beautiful section, nature and our people have worked together to produce a lovely and tranquil Town." There is no mention of the horror that had taken place there during one hot summer; the lives that were lost. The first to die on that gloriously sunny afternoon as the town was preparing for its annual Moose Festival was thirty-two-year-old New Hampshire State Trooper Scott E. Phillips. Trooper Phillips was a fit young man with tightly cropped black hair and a big gap-toothed smile. Though born along the sandy beaches of Cape Cod, Phillips was a true son of New Hampshire, having been raised in Lancaster, where he attended school before graduating White Mountains Regional High School in 1984. Phillips quickly turned in his diploma for a rifle and joined the U.S. Army, serving in its military police until his discharge in 1989. He returned to Lancaster, joined the state police, and made a quiet life for himself, his wife Christine, and their young boys Keenan and Clancy. Scott Phillips was also civic-minded: he volunteered for the Special Olympics Torch Run every year, carrying the flame through his hometown.

Trooper Phillips had no idea of the searing resentment inside Carl Drega's soul, or how it would be unleashed on that fateful summer day. Drega's sister would later tell reporters that her brother claimed he'd been a longtime victim of harassment from police and town officials. It "got to the point where he couldn't take it any more," Jane Drega said. The internal torment had been building since the 1970s, when Carl Drega found himself at odds with local officials about whether he could tarpaper his home. A few years later, Drega, a carpenter who worked occasionally over the border at the Vermont Yankee nuclear power plant, angered town fathers again by dumping a ton of dirt along a riverbank on his land. He had claimed that a recent rainstorm had washed away eighty feet of his property and that he was simply trying to restore the lot to its original size. State officials didn't see it that way, however; they argued that Drega was intent on diverting the course of the Connecticut River. The locals knew what Carl Drega was capable of. He had been locked in a test of will with what he determined to be the small town's "power brokers" for years. Colebrook residents caught a glimpse of his violent potential in 1995, when local attorney Vickie Bunnell tried to mediate a dispute between Drega and a local tax assessor. As Bunnell approached his home, Drega fired a volley of shots in the air and chased her off his property. The gunshots were a warning to Bunnell and anyone else in Colebrook that it was best to leave Carl Drega alone. After the showdown with Bunnell, Drega outfitted his property with early warning electronic noise and motion detectors. He also purchased a high-powered rifle and a bulletproof vest.

That warning didn't deter Trooper Scott Phillips, who had noticed an old red pickup truck pockmarked with gaping holes of rust in its bed entering the parking lot of LaPerle's IGA supermarket. The vehicle looked barely drivable to the young trooper. No doubt it was a potential hazard to its owner and anyone he shared the road with. Phillips pulled into the lot with the intent of citing the rust bucket's driver while another trooper, forty-five-year-old Leslie G. Lord, drove in after him. Trooper Lord had been in law enforcement for more than twenty years, having once served as police chief of his hometown of Pittsburg, New Hampshire, before eventually joining the state police. He'd also been the fire chief of his local fire department and a loving husband to his wife Beverly and doting father to their two sons Corey and Shawn.

What began as a mundane traffic citation quickly dissolved into the bloodiest day in the history of this quiet, rural area. As Trooper Phillips approached Drega's red rust bucket, he was confronted with the business end of an AR-15 automatic rifle. Carl Drega pulled the trigger, immediately striking Phillips in the hand. The young trooper returned fire but was unable to penetrate Drega's protective vest. Watching in horror as the gunfight played out before his eyes, Trooper Lord jumped out of his police cruiser to help. Lord was shot and killed before his feet hit the ground. With deadly and detached efficiency, Drega turned his attention back to Trooper Phillips, who although wounded had tried to climb a nearby embankment for cover. Drega strolled up to the injured trooper and shot him four times at close range with a 9 mm pistol—execution style. Drega then took Phillips's own bulletproof vest, commandeered the trooper's vehicle, and drove into town.

It would come as no surprise that his next stop was Vickie Bunnell's law office inside a building at 1 Bridge Street. The former selectman turned part-time judge had been scared off Drega's property two years before, and knew exactly the danger she was facing now. Bunnell pushed her secretary out a back door to safety and then ran into the adjacent office of *The News and Sentinel*, Colebrook's weekly newspaper, to alert others. "It's Drega!" she screamed. "He's got a gun!" By this time, Carl Drega had positioned himself near the back door. He watched silently as Bunnell attempted to flee the building and shot her in the back while the woman was in midstride. Dennis Joos, the fifty-year-old editor of the *News and Sentinel*, ran outside unarmed and tried to tackle the gunman, but the six-foot-three, 240-pound Drega simply dragged Joos about fifteen feet, threw him on the hood of the car, and shot him several times. The madman got back into the police vehicle and next called upon a local selectman, who fortunately was not at home when Drega kicked his front door in. Carl Drega knew it would only be a matter of minutes before every available law enforcement official in the North Country descended on his dilapidated homestead, and he wanted to make sure they received a terrifying welcome. He returned home and set the place ablaze with diesel fuel he had purchased earlier in the day. Drega's rage had not yet been satisfied. He then drove across the state line into Vermont, where he took a shot at New Hampshire Fish and Game officer Wayne Saunders. Fortunately, the projectile ricocheted off Saunders's badge and penetrated his arm but caused no serious damage. Carl Drega shot and wounded two more officers, a border agent and a Vermont state trooper before a posse of more than twenty policemen closed in. Still armed with an AR-15 and 150 rounds of ammunition, Drega opened fire once more but this time he didn't stand a chance. He was shot and killed by a bullet through the mouth. Carl Drega was now dead but he was still quite dangerous. Police spent several more days sifting through the booby trap–laden remnants of his burned-out home: they discovered six more rifles, eighty-six pipe bombs and explosives, and projectile casings for a grenade launcher.

Publisher John Harrigan, whose parents owned the *News and Sentinel*, wrote an editorial later that evening that read in part, "God love these people as their families and their towns did and God help us all deal with what has happened, and remember those fine cherished faces, and their smiles." The editorial ran under the headline "Horrible, Unbelievable and Other Words That Fail." John Harrigan, however, had the perfect words to describe Carl Drega. "He was just a piece of space junk that happened to get us," he told reporters. "It was our turn."

The state of New Hampshire had virtually no time to recover from the rampage in Colebrook. No more than five days after the momentous tragedy, another officer would also be gunned down in the line of duty: Jeremy T. Charron. Charron was just twenty-four and in his first year as a patrolman for the Epsom, New Hampshire, police department; like Scott E. Phillips, he was a veteran of the armed forces. Charron had served a four-year stint in the U.S. Marine Corps after graduating Hillsborough-Deering High School in 1992. The third of Bob and Fran Charron's five children, Jeremy was a classic overachiever from early on. He played tenacious defense on the high school soccer team and had been voted president of his senior class. Charron had always dreamed of a career in law enforcement and hoped one day to join the New Hampshire state police. He was now laying down the groundwork to achieve that goal. Charron had been promoted to full-time officer status in Epsom, a town made up predominantly of farmland, just six miles long from border to border; he was also taking criminal justice courses at the New Hampshire Technical College in Concord.

On the last day of his life, Charron's own thoughts were of the troopers who had recently been murdered in Colebrook. He had not known either Scott E. Phillips or Leslie G. Lord, but he mourned them as fallen brothers and had spent the previous day attending both their funerals. Jeremy Charron was working the graveyard shift on the morning of August 24, 1997, when he was asked to check out a report of a suspicious vehicle in Webster Park, a popular swimming hole where the Epsom Town Band played its annual summer concert series. Charron approached the car and found two men, twenty-two-year-old Gordon Perry and nineteen-year-old Kevin Paul, sleeping inside. The officer tapped on the glass on the driver's-side window and asked the pair for the car's registration certificate and both their driver's licenses. Perry, an ex-con, obliged with the request, handed over the paperwork, and stepped out of the vehicle. As Charron began to question him about exactly what he was doing in the park at five in the morning, Gordon Perry pulled out a gun and fired several shots at the officer, most of the bullets getting absorbed by his protective vest. One bullet, however, struck Charron in the side and traveled deep into his chest. Despite his grave wound, Jeremy Charron managed to pull his service weapon out of its holster and fire several rounds of his own before he collapsed to the ground. A few of the shots hit the suspects' car as the men made their getaway. Perry and Paul quickly ditched the car, stole a pickup truck, and robbed a convenience store as they continued their escape.

By now, virtually every police officer in New Hampshire had gotten word of the shooting. Most were still wearing black armbands on their uniforms when they joined the pursuit for New Hampshire's latest cop killers. The wanted men traveled north, using mostly the southbound lanes of Interstate 93 pushing the truck's speed to 80 mph while oncoming drivers swerved to avoid them. Gordon and Perry were "quite literally aiming toward the vehicles that were coming toward them," New Hampshire Attorney General Philip McLaughlin later told reporters. "They were not attempting to evade those vehicles. Thankfully, oncoming cars were able to avoid them." The chase ended when the men crashed the stolen pickup truck on the median of I-93 in Bethlehem, New Hampshire, about eighty miles north of Epsom. One suspect was arrested at the scene; the other was chased down in some nearby woods. Kevin Paul received a prison sentence of fifteen to sixty years for the murder of Officer Jeremy Charron, while triggerman Gordon Perry got life behind bars. Among those who served as pallbearers at Charron's funeral was Manchester police officer Michael Briggs. The cruel irony does not end there: included in the list of officers later honored with a Certificate of Special Congressional Recognition for their roles in the capture of Charron's killers was Bruce McKay.

❦ The day after Bruce McKay was shot and killed, Governor John Lynch ordered all American and state flags lowered to half-staff. He also traveled up to Franconia to get a firsthand sense of the collective mood of the townspeople. There is little doubt that Lynch heard whispers about the troubled history between McKay and his killer. Still, the governor made sure the public knew where his sympathies lay. In a prepared statement, Lynch said, "This terrible tragedy has impacted families, the Franconia area and the entire state of New Hampshire. My thoughts and prayers, and those of my wife, Susan, are with the family of Cpl. McKay, whose courage, service and commitment to protecting others is an example for us all." Attorney General Kelly Ayotte, State Police Captain Russell Conte, and Senior Assistant Attorney General Jeffrey Strelzin were also in Franconia, giving reporters a summary of the deadly encounter. They claimed that Liko Kenney had been pulled over for speeding and a problem with his car's registration. Only the latter is true. Corporal McKay had made no mention to dispatch of just how fast the Toyota Celica was traveling, or to Liko Kenney when he finally had pulled him over. Attorney General Ayotte did say that Bruce McKay's murder had been captured by the dash-cam video in his police cruiser and that the officer had not been wearing his protective vest. Her assistant, Jeffrey Strelzin, also stressed that McKay used a "small amount of force, not excessive" to push Liko Kenney's Celica off the road. Strelzin's comment would later be called into question when the public got its first look at the video-tape. Kelly Ayotte said that Bruce McKay had been shot four times in the "upper trunk" although she admitted that she had not seen the full autopsy report.

Kelly Ayotte had cut her teeth on homicide cases like this one. The confident, attractive brunette had served as lead prosecu-tor in the case against two Vermont teenagers in what would be known as "The Dartmouth Murders." Seventeen-year-old Robert Tulloch and sixteen-year-old James Parker had been accused of slaying two Dartmouth College professors in their Hanover, New Hampshire, home in 2001. The teens had talked their way into the home of Half and Susanne Zantop, posing as students taking an environmental survey. They then butchered the couple with a pair of footlong commando knives. Kelly Ayotte, then senior assistant attorney general, told the jury the boys had become bored with life in their rural hometown of Chelsea, Vermont, and wanted to steal enough money to move to Australia. The teens began their quest by stealing mail from people's houses; when that didn't work, Tulloch decided it would be more profitable to jump people and kill them for their bank cards. Ayotte said the teens targeted nearby Hanover, New Hampshire, because residents had a lot of money and they especially targeted the Zantops' home because it looked "expensive." Tulloch and Parker murdered the couple by slitting their throats.

There was little "reasonable doubt" going into the trials. These killers were as clumsy as they were deadly. They left behind the knife sheaths, which helped investigators identify them through sales records. Authorities also found Half Zantop's blood in Parker's car and prints matching his shoe and Robert Tulloch's finger at the crime scene. Both were arrested at an Indiana truck stop two days after the murders. Robert Tulloch was later found guilty and sentenced to life without parole, while James Parker cut a deal to testify against his friend. He is now serving twenty-five years to life. Following the cases of *State v. Tulloch* and *State v. Parker*, Ayotte left the attorney general's office briefly to serve as legal counsel for New Hampshire Governor Craig Benson before returning to the office in July 2003 when she was appointed deputy attorney general. Kelly Ayotte would become the state's first female attorney general just one year later.

With two police shootings in the past seven months, Ayotte now faced her biggest challenge as the state's top prosecutor. The murder of Manchester police officer Michael Briggs appeared to be cut-and-dried. There was not even a hint of sympathy toward his killer, Michael "Styx" Addison. It was quickly becoming evident to all that the story unfolding in Franconia was markedly different. The gunman in this case was not an outsider. As described by his uncle, Liko Kenney was in fact a "son of the valley." Bruce McKay, on the other hand, was not. He was a "flatlander" from Long Island, New York, who despite having called New Hampshire home, was not considered "one of us" by many locals. Possibly sensing a growing animosity toward McKay, Kelly Ayotte continued to stress the image of a fallen hero. Her demeanor and comments reflected those of Governor John Lynch. "This is a terrible loss to our state," she told the gathered media. "It once again reminds us of the difficult and dangerous work that is done every day by law enforcement of the state to protect each of us. The police officers of the state, including Corporal McKay, are nothing short of heroes."

So far, little was known about the so-called courageous stranger who had happened upon the murder of a police officer and had then proceeded to take justice into his own hands. Eleanor Lovett, a clerk at the Franconia Village Store told the *Concord Monitor* that Greg Floyd had waltzed into the Franconia Village Store two days after the shooting looking for the Sunday newspaper. Lovett told Floyd they were all sold out. "I'm the guy who shot that kid," he reportedly boasted. Lovett said Floyd had a breezy demeanor, as if he'd shot a rabbit.

During her news conference on May 12, Attorney General Ayotte had said that Floyd's actions appeared to be a "justified use of deadly force" and that no criminal charges were expected against him. As standard practice in cases such as this, authorities usually will refuse to rule out any further actions against any involved parties pending the outcome of their investigation. Ayotte's speedy decision to absolve Floyd of any wrongdoing is peculiar, given the amount of prescription drugs in his system, his violent past, and the fact he was forbidden by law from using a firearm.

Gregory Willis Floyd had first come to the attention of New Hampshire authorities shortly after moving to Easton with his wife Michelle and their son Gregory in January 1997. The couple had lived previously at a condominium complex in Townsend, Massachusetts, where Floyd was remembered as a difficult neighbor. "To me, he [Floyd] was as bad as the guy he shot," says Calvin Robbins, property manager for Country Estates, a twenty-three-unit building where the Floyds lived. "I had major problems with him." Robbins claims Floyd once cut down several trees without his approval in an effort to let more sunlight into his unit. He also claims that Floyd would never turn the heat up in his unit; instead, he would crank up the heat in the hallway and open his door to let the warm air blow in. "When he got his disability settlement (for a back injury he had received while working as a carpenter for Lone Star Sanville in Ayer, Massachusetts) he bought a place in New Hampshire and I said good riddance," Robbins recalls. As gun enthusiasts, Greg and Michelle Floyd both wanted a place deep in the woods where they could fire weapons without opening themselves up to the encroachment and hassle of local cops. The Floyds thought they had found such a place on Hummingbird Lane, a quiet, winding, one-lane road dotted by a few tucked-away homes. Their cabin was surrounded by thick pines and a long driveway that led back to the road. They felt isolated, which was fine with them. Greg Floyd had turned his back on the outside world, following two felony convictions for selling marijuana in the state of Georgia in 1981. In the years to come, Greg Floyd would several times place himself at odds with the law.

In late April 1997, officials at the Lafayette Regional School asked police to check on the welfare of young Gregory Paul Floyd; they had received a report that the boy's father was shooting weapons on his property and that one of the bullets had struck a nearby house on Hummingbird Lane. Bob Every, the Easton police chief, drove out to Hummingbird Lane and spoke first with Floyd's neighbors. The bullet in question had struck the side of Alma Jean Boisvert's home, just 400 feet from Floyd's property. Boisvert and her husband told Every that they had not reported the incident because they were trying to be "good neighbors." The Boisverts did tell the police chief that Floyd seemed "strange" and that there was "more to him than meets the eye."

The couple downplayed the shooting and said that their neighbor had apologized and had told them he did not realize their house was so close to his. Chief Every accepted the explanation, but deep down he sensed they were more than nervous about Greg Floyd's presence on Hummingbird Lane. Chief Every next drove to Greg Floyd's cabin and spoke with Michelle Floyd, who met him at the door but did not invite him in. "My husband's not home," she told him. They chatted for about five minutes and that was enough time for Bob Every to determine Floyd's young son was not in any apparent danger.

Nearly two weeks later on May 12, 1997, Floyd's other neighbors, Betty and Maurice Rodrigue, traveled to Chief Every's home and told him they had heard Greg Floyd shooting in the past and that it sounded to them like an automatic weapon. Betty Rodrigue also told the chief that she had heard Greg Floyd had an arrest record for violent behavior. Chief Every ran a record check on Floyd and also reached out to his colleagues in Townsend and Chelmsford, Massachusetts, where the Floyds had previously resided. Chelmsford police were unable to find any records on Greg Floyd. The Townsend police chief told Every that he did not know whether Floyd had automatic weapons but did remember that he was capable of irrational behavior. "Be careful on making any approach," he advised.

Chief Every returned to Hummingbird Lane for more questioning. The Rodrigues told him they'd heard Floyd shoot on three separate occasions—all at night. On the first occasion, Floyd told the couple he was scaring away some bears so that his son could sleep. The second time, Betty Rodrigue was startled by a burst of about fifteen shots. She wasn't a gun woman but she had fired a weapon before. She didn't think it was possible to pull the trigger that fast. "It has to be an automatic weapon," she told Every. On the third occasion, the couple heard three individual heavy-caliber rounds. "He's paranoid when he takes medication," they said. "Floyd gets excited to the point where you can't understand what he's saying." The Rodrigues also noted that Floyd had begun to put a locked chain across his driveway and that he kept it locked whether he was there or not.

Bob Every later approached the Boisverts and found them much more willing to talk this time around. They told him they had heard gunshots coming from the Floyd residence on three occasions but that they were all during the day and all on different dates from the ones their neighbors had described. The last had occurred the day after Every had initially spoken to the Boisverts and Floyd's wife. In a wild rage, Greg Floyd had accused the couple of sending the police chief to his home. According to the Boisverts, Floyd tried turning the tables and accusing them of shooting at *his* house. Again, Chief Every sensed fear from Floyd's neighbors. He also had probable cause to believe Greg Floyd had an automatic weapon. In his affidavit in support of a search warrant for Floyd's home, Chief Bob Every wrote: "All of us make mistakes in our lives; in Mr. Floyd's case the behavior extends beyond a mistake; there is a pattern, a pattern of past violence, paranoid behavior, and excessive anger. While no one can predict the future, I feel Mr. Floyd is capable of showing up at the Lafayette Elementary School or at a neighbor's house with an automatic weapon and that the danger to public safety far outweighs the minimal intrusion a check of his premises for automatic weapons would represent." Chief Every also stated he felt the state police were better equipped and trained to carry out the search warrant than he was. He also asked the court to keep his affidavit sealed "because of Mr. Floyd's nature."

On May 19, 1997, New Hampshire state troopers searched Floyd's home at 101 Hummingbird Lane and discovered the following weapons:

1 Merwin Herbert .32 cal.
2 Glock 9 mm
3 Ithaca 12-gauge shotgun
4 Ruger Model 233
5 Ruger Black Hawk
6 Black Power San Marco

None of the six weapons were automatic. Floyd allowed the troopers into his home without incident. As he handed over the Merwin Herbet .32 caliber pistol, Floyd told one state trooper: "When I was shooting I shot at a tree. I shot it twice and hit it both times. I can show you where it is. I am an ex-Marine and an expert shot. I don't miss what I shoot at." According to the official New Hampshire State Police Criminal Investigation report, the search was conducted without incident and that the case was closed. What officials did not realize was that they had stirred up the hornet's nest and that it would be only a matter of time before the agitated hornet struck back.

Shay Littlefield was ill-prepared for his encounter with Greg Floyd just one day after state troopers had searched the man's home. Littlefield, a meter reader for Field Tech, had parked on the side of Hummingbird Lane because of the long iron chain across the driveway. Littlefield climbed out of his company vehicle and walked toward the house to read the meter. The worker made a few notes and was returning to his truck when Floyd came barreling out of his front door with his dog close at his heels. The animal began barking loudly and ran off in the direction of the now terrified meter reader. Floyd gave the dog a verbal command of some kind and it immediately broke off the chase.

"What the fuck are you doing here?" Floyd yelled.

"Reading the meter, same as always," Littlefield responded nervously.

"Why didn't you honk before coming into the yard?"

"I will the next time," Littlefield replied.

"My dog is trained to attack the throat and groin," Greg Floyd warned.

Shay Littlefield informed him that he had mace and would protect himself if the dog attacked.

"That dog is worth $2,000 and you'll be shot if you hurt the dog!" Floyd promised, growing angrier by the minute. He then marched up and stood nose to nose with the meter reader. "Do I need to kick your ass?" Floyd barked as his fists tightened. "Go get the pouch!" he yelled back to his son. Gregory ran into the house but returned just moments later. "Mom is awake and I couldn't get the gun," he told his father. That was Shay Littlefield's cue to get the hell out of there. Littlefield drove straight to the Easton Police Department and filed a criminal complaint.

Two New Hampshire State Troopers, Bret Beausoleil and Scott Bryan, drove up to Floyd's home after learning of the complaint a few weeks later. This time they had a warrant for the man's arrest. As they made their way up the driveway, Michelle Floyd came out to the front porch. "What do you want?" she asked. The troopers told her they were looking for Greg Floyd. The shirtless man exited the home and joined his wife on the front porch where he was told there was a warrant for his arrest for criminal threatening and that the alleged victim was the meter reader.

"That fucking pussy," Floyd said, shaking his head. "We just talked to his boss and they indicated things would be taken care of, and they would honk the next time. I wanna file my own complaint for criminal trespassing and I wanna do it right now!" Trooper Beausoleil told Floyd that it would be a conflict of interest for them to investigate and prosecute both sides of the same incident, but that he was welcome to file his complaint with another trooper. Greg Floyd invited the officers in and offered to call Shay Littlefield's supervisor to get the whole thing straightened out. "You can do that later," Trooper Bryan said. "Right now you're coming with us."

Those words sent Greg Floyd into a frenzy. "If you're going to take me you better get my Valium, barbiturates, and a number of other painkillers because I'm gonna get fucked up!" Floyd continued on in a ramble of curses and threats against the troopers. "My dog is trained to attack the throat, if I had wanted to he would have attacked you! . . . Fucking 'Live Free or Die,' this state has no constitutional rights! . . . I could have given you a third eye. . . . I know you wear a vest so I would have put it right between your eyes. I was sitting on my Ruger." Floyd then turned his vitriol back to meter reader Shay Littlefield. "Why can't men be men? I want to take that pussy out in the woods and settle it in the mud and blood! If that pussy comes back, or if I see him again I'll kill him!"

Several times during his murderous soliloquy, Floyd paused to point out what a traumatic effect the troopers' presence was having on his son. Following a fifteen-minute harangue, Greg Floyd was finally allowed to take his pain medication. Trooper Bryan then ordered him to get a shirt and some shoes for the ride to the state police barracks. Bryan was forced to cuff Floyd in the front because of his back injuries; while he was doing so, Floyd attempted to knee him in the groin. Bryan brushed off the attack and double-locked the handcuffs. As he was being escorted out to the police cruiser, Floyd yelled to his son. "Look at the fucking pigs! Aren't they big men? Look and see what they are like and don't forget it!"

Greg Floyd posted $150 bail and was driven back home by the troopers. "I could have given you a third eye," he reiterated as they approached his log cabin. Floyd later pleaded guilty to assaulting Trooper Bryan by attempting to knee him in the groin. He faced one to three years in prison but instead received a suspended sentence. Following the incident, authorities conducted a deeper background check and discovered the two felony convictions in Georgia. The convictions meant Floyd could not lawfully own any firearms. Why such a background check was not done a month prior when he was accused of shooting on his property remains a mystery. Floyd had been arrested on another occasion in Georgia when he and three others had been accused of stealing two two-foot statues, one of the Virgin Mary, the other of Saint Francis of Assissi, from a person's property. The statues had each been worth more than one hundred dollars. Floyd was ordered to pay a $250.00 fine and a restitution of $37.50 plus court costs.

On the afternoon of July 24, 1997, Bret Beausoleil and three other state troopers executed an arrest warrant and search warrant at Greg Floyd's home. The ex-Marine's driveway was locked with a chain, so Trooper Beausoleil called Floyd on his cell phone and asked him to meet them at the locked cable. The request was denied. The search team waited another fifteen minutes for Floyd to come out on his own accord. When nothing happened, they went in after him. The troopers found Greg Floyd on the phone with Gina Appicelli, a Woodsville attorney. Floyd allowed one of the men, Trooper Robert Bruno, to speak with *his* attorney, who told the trooper that she did not represent Mr. Floyd and that he had just called her office upon their arrival. Appicelli reportedly told the trooper to hang up the phone and make the arrest.

Bruno explained why the warrants had been issued, but Floyd protested, "I told Massachusetts authorities about my drug problems but they issued me a firearms identification card." He retrieved his card and one issued to Michelle. Both had been issued by the town of Chelmsford in 1987. Trooper Bruno told the Floyds that Massachusetts officials were wrong to issue him a firearms identification card; as a convicted felon he was not allowed to possess any kind of gun.

"We both belong to a gun club in Massachusetts," Michelle Floyd announced.

"Have you seen your husband use firearms?" Trooper Bruno asked. Michelle Floyd nodded yes but said she'd only seen him shoot in Massachusetts. "Does he handle guns around the house?"

"He's cleaned a gun."

Bruno told Michelle that her husband wasn't even allowed to clean a gun or have control of a gun. As his conversation with Mrs. Floyd continued, Bruno's state police colleagues began a full search of the home, beginning in the kitchen where they found an Ithaca shotgun on top of a cupboard along with a loaded .32 caliber revolver. A search of the master bedroom uncovered a San Marco Black Power .50 caliber rifle and a Glock with three magazines on top of a bedroom bureau. A Ruger Super Black Hawk .44 magnum handgun and holster were found on the floor, to the right side of Floyd's bed. An unknown 6.5 caliber rifle was located in a bedroom closet and a Ruger Mini 14 was found on a box-spring mattress in the master bedroom. Michelle Floyd insisted the cache belonged to her, despite referring several times to "my husband's guns." During the time of the search, Greg Floyd was handcuffed and secure in the backseat of a police cruiser. He was joined outside by Gregory, who had pedaled his bicycle down the driveway to meet him.

"Are they [the troopers] beating up your mother?" Greg Sr. asked the boy. "Are they stealing anything?" A devilish grin then spread across Greg Floyd's face. "Go get the Claymore Clappers," he told his son. "Let's blow the place."

Greg Floyd's home was still standing as he was driven away to the Littleton, New Hampshire, police department, where he was booked, photographed, and fingerprinted. Floyd spoke freely as Trooper Bruno announced that he was going to advise him of his rights. This didn't seem to matter to Floyd, who rambled on that his wife's constitutional rights were being violated and he was a veteran, having served in the Marine Corps from 1976 to 1985.

"Didn't they [the Marine Corps] have a problem with the drug conviction?" Bruno asked.

"Absolutely not," Floyd replied. "I was in the NSA, the No Such Agency." Floyd told the trooper that this agency was more powerful than the CIA and that he had been stationed in South America."

"Whatd'ya do in South America?"

"You are now in a top secret area," Floyd warned the trooper, saying no more about his military career, real or imagined. Bruno later checked into Greg Floyd's military background and found that he had served in the Marine Corps from February 27, 1976, to February 26, 1979, and that he had received an honorable discharge after three years. This appeared to be the only fact in Floyd's fictional account of his military past. According to the National Personnel Records Center in St. Louis, Missouri, Floyd had done no overseas duty and had received no decorations or awards. Instead, he had performed his tour of duty at Camp Lejune, North Carolina, where he was assigned to staff headquarters. Floyd's military service was unremarkable. In fact, he didn't leave an impression with anyone. What Floyd's actual duties were remains unclear, but when Trooper Bruno asked officials whether Floyd's claim of being Force Recon was highly inflated, the answer was yes. Bruno also discovered that Floyd had gone AWOL on two occasions.

When it came time for meter reader Shay Littlefield to testify against Greg Floyd at trial in October 1997, the plaintiff startled investigators when he told them that he wasn't sure whether he could identify Floyd in open court. The defendant had arrived at the courthouse that day hobbling on a pair of crutches, showing great difficulty as he tried to walk. Littlefield had remembered that Floyd had been much more spritely on the day several months earlier when the ex-Marine had threatened to kill him. Whether Floyd used the crutches as a defense prop to elicit sympathy or whether he was truly in pain because of his back problems cannot be known. Whatever the case, it certainly paid off. Following her cross-examination of Shay Littlefield, Floyd's attorney made an oral motion to dismiss the case because the meter reader could not identify the defendant for certain. The judge then asked the prosecutor whether he intended to call Floyd's son to the witness stand. It was Gregory Floyd who had been told to go back in the house and "get the pouch." The State said it would not call the young boy to the stand, so the judge granted the defense motion to dismiss the case. The gun charges against Greg Floyd were also eventually dismissed by the Grafton, New Hampshire, county attorney's office because it determined the charges did not meet the legal standards necessary to support prosecution.

❧ Greg Floyd's ghosts still haunted him a decade later when he pulled the trigger ending Liko Kenney's life near the Easton town line. He was at ease discussing his service background with witnesses and investigators at the crime scene and later at the state police barracks. Floyd's total number of kills had bounced around from twenty-three to forty-three. How much of his past glory is only in his mind has yet to be determined, but what cannot be debated is Floyd's willingness to kill with impunity. In the shooting death of Liko Kenney, the New Hampshire attorney general's office determined it was carried out in accordance to state law which "permits an actor who is not a law enforcement officer to use deadly force when the actor reasonably believes that another is about to use deadly force against the actor or a third person. The phrase 'reasonably believes' means the actor 'need not have been confronted with actual deadly peril, as long as he could reasonably believe the peril to be real.'"

Another precedent considered in the Floyd case was *Aldrich v. Wright*, 53 N.H. 398 (1893), in which a defendant killed minks to protect his geese "notwithstanding the existence of a statute providing that "no person shall in any way destroy . . . any mink, . . . under penalty of ten dollars for each animal so destroyed." Applied more than a century later to the Liko Kenney shooting, it meant that the actor's conduct should be viewed "under circumstances as they were presented to him at the time, and not necessarily as they appear upon detached reflection." What prosecutors failed to consider, however, was Floyd's state of mind at the time of shooting. Having digested a potent cocktail of twenty-two prescription drugs, Greg Floyd was susceptible to hallucinations and overactive reflexes that could have seriously altered his ability to determine what was and what was not deemed a serious threat.

But I have promises to keep,
and miles to go before I sleep,
and miles to go before I sleep.
ROBERT FROST

The morning skies were thick with fog, befitting the dark mood of the day. The high-pitched moans of bagpipes and the thunder of marching feet reverberated through Franconia Notch as hundreds of police officers from around the nation walked lockstep toward Echo Lake at the base of Cannon Mountain. Some followed on horseback; still others, on motorcycles. All had worn a black ribbon over their shield and all had come to pay tribute to another one of their own killed in the line of duty. It was a reluctant pilgrimage borne out of honor for the badge and honor for a brother-in-arms. No police officer wanted to be here, but all felt they had to be. Most had gone to great lengths to attend; in fact officers in Portland, Maine, would later be investigated for allegedly using their sirens and flashing lights to make better time during the drive to neighboring New Hampshire for the funeral. Only a few dozen officers had known Bruce McKay in life; in death, however, his name would be remembered by hundreds, if not thousands of his comrades, who knew all too well they too could leave for work one day and only to never return home. Oftentimes there are steep prices to be paid for attaining a level of authority. Today was one of those times. The pageantry of the funeral cortege was as breathtakingly beautiful as it was horribly sad. Officers in their dress blues formed a continuous wave of tribute under a blanket of clouds hanging low off the surrounding mountains. Residents of the small, tight-knit community held small American flags as they stood in the rain by the roadside while the hearse carrying Bruce McKay's casket passed slowly by.

The previous day's scene had been just as dramatic, when Corporal McKay's flag-draped coffin had been placed in the Franconia Town Hall for two public viewings. Resting on top of the coffin was McKay's police hat, next to a white satin heart-shaped pillow that held his badge. A rotating honor guard made up of police officers and firefighters stood vigil over the coffin as streams of mourners wound their way through the town hall toward the casket carrying the body of one of their own. The Franconia Police Department's two remaining full-time officers both wore gold-accented dress uniforms that had been designed by McKay shortly before his murder for occasions just like this one. A collage of police photos stood in front of the coffin with a small sign reading, OUR FINEST. More than a dozen local motel owners and innkeepers, including Sue and Chet Thompson, offered discount rates to those attending the services from out of town. The Thompsons made only one condition: that guests not discuss the incident, owing to the close proximity between the crime scene and the Kinsman Lodge. McKay's younger sister Meggen Payerle had flown up from Maryland with her husband, Andy. The whole affair had seemed so surreal to her. It was as if she were playing a role in someone else's tragedy. Only a few days before, she had heard a knock on the front door of her suburban home at 2 A.M. Andy answered the door; on the other side was a police officer. The officer had asked to come inside and insisted that he speak with Meggen. "I have some bad news," he told her. Somehow Meggen understood immediately. "You're here to tell me that my brother's dead." Bruce's sister had been waiting for this day for years, dreading it. "I always knew that he wouldn't lead a long life," she recalls. Meggen felt that his adventurous spirit would one day cause his demise. She swallowed the tragic news and tried focusing on the logistics of getting where she needed to be. She and her husband had been planning a vacation to the beach; now they found themselves preparing to travel north to her brother's funeral. Bruce McKay's comrades offered their assistance along the way. The couple received a police escort from their Adamstown, Maryland, home all the way to Franconia, New Hampshire. It was at that moment that Meggen finally understood the power of the brotherhood. Her brother had talked about it before calling his fellow officers his "extended family," but now she was seeing it firsthand and this incredible show of support allowed her to finally cry for Bruce. She had kept her emotions tucked deep inside for the first six to eight hours, but now she was letting it all out.

While Meggen was trying to come to grips with her own emotions, Bruce's fiancée Sharon Davis was facing a different challenge: renewed tensions between her and McKay's former wife Angela. According to Sharon, Angela had accused her of stealing Bruce's Saint Michael's medallion off his body. "It was ridiculous," says Sharon. "The only thing I took from Bruce was a Seiko watch that I'd given him as an engagement present." Sharon claims the accusation was part of a scheme by Angela to portray herself as McKay's true grieving widow. It may be impossible to judge Angela's motives but her accusations rose to the level of action the day following the funeral; she filed a court order to bar Sharon and Bruce's father from his Landaff home.

Another battle was being waged outside the family by friends who stood up to defend Bruce's memory, which had suddenly been called into question. "Bruce has shown nothing but kindness to my family," Melissa Devoe-Stephenson told a reporter from the Associated Press. McKay had been one of the first emergency responders when Stephenson's first husband had been killed in a road rage incident. "Bruce McKay was the first one on the scene of the accident and had offered my husband moments of comfort and kindness right before he died, so we have nothing but the utmost respect for Bruce." The family of McKay's killer also released a statement of sympathy for the family of Bruce McKay: "The Kenney-Miller family would like to take this opportunity to extend our sincere sorrow about the incident that happened and send out our condolences first and foremost to the daughter and family of Officer McKay and also the friends and greater law enforcement community, and just want to recognize the pain that they're feeling."

There was no talk about Liko Kenney or the Kenney-Miller family at Bruce McKay's funeral on the following day. The passions that had been ignited by both men were allowed to cool for a brief period of time while the focus turned rightly to arguably the most tragic victim of this violent affair: Bruce's nine-year-old daughter, Courtney. Not only had she lost her father and primary caregiver, she had also lost her best friend. What goes through a young girl's mind when she realizes that her daddy is gone forever? It is safe to assume that Courtney and those around her thought deeply about those cherished moments they had spent together and those moments he would not be there for. Bruce McKay would never meet Courtney's first boyfriend. He would not be there when she would raise her high school and college diplomas triumphantly over her head. He would not be there to give his daughter away on her wedding day. Dressed smartly in a white skirt with blue paisley prints, her brown hair not yet lightened by the summer sun, Courtney stood up before her family members, her father's friends and comrades, and New Hampshire governor John Lynch to deliver the eulogy: "You knew my dad as Franconia Officer Bruce McKay or 44-K," Courtney said with a slight lisp, her tender voice cracking under the emotional weight of the moment. "But he was so much more than that."

Nine-year-old Courtney could read no more. Staring out at the thousands of faces that had been leaning forward to hear her words, the only face she longed to see was her father's. The child realized she could not continue and the Reverend Lyn Winter was asked to finish the eulogy. The voice was the reverend's, but the sentiment belonged to Courtney McKay: "He loved nature, he loved our house, he loved being a police officer and he loved me. We went fishing, we went motorcycle riding and we especially liked taking naps together. My dad was the greatest and bravest man

I have ever known. My love for him will never die." Courtney McKay was embraced by Governor John Lynch, who told her, "Seeing you in such sadness causes our collective hearts to break as well." The governor followed those words with a message to all the mourners and the community beyond. "An attack on a police officer is an attack on all of us." Officials also presented a state award to Meggen Payerle and Sharon Davis. The award was to have been given to Bruce the following week for making an arrest that led investigators to a widespread fraud ring. Former Portledge School classmate and longtime friend Special Forces Lt. Colonel Adrian Bogart also attended the service. Bogart had been awarded the Bronze Star after serving as chief of staff/executive officer for the Combined Joint Special Operations Task Force in Afghanistan and later in Iraq where he was responsible for Special Operations Forces integration and counterinsurgency. "We had planned to go hiking in the White Mountains one day when our schedules would allow," Bogart told the *Union Leader*. "That day did not come." He called his dear friend an "American hero" as he placed his Bronze Star on Bruce McKay's casket.

The service closed with the sound of gunshots fired by state police officers in honor of Bruce McKay from a knoll behind a large white tent where the funeral had been held. A bugler played taps and a famous poem by Franconia's iconic poet laureate Robert Frost was recited.

The Road Not Taken
Two roads diverged in a yellow wood,
And sorry I could not travel both,
And be one traveler, long I stood,
And looked down one as far as I could
To where it bent in the undergrowth;

Then took the other, as just as fair,
And having perhaps the better claim,
Because it was grassy and wanted wear,

Though as for that the passing there,
Had worn them really about the same,

And both that morning equally lay,
In leaves no step had trodden black.
Oh, I kept the first for another day!
Yet knowing how way leads onto way,
I doubted if I should ever come back.

I shall be telling this with a sigh
Somewhere ages and ages hence:
Two roads diverged in a wood, and I—
I took the one less traveled by,
And that has made all the difference.

The slight drizzle was replaced by a steady downpour when the community gathered to remember Liko Kenney two days after Bruce McKay's funeral. The sky was colorless and heavy with precipitation. The only light came from the brightly colored umbrellas carried by hundreds of mourners to the grounds of the Tamarack Tennis Camp. They huddled under a small white tent in the field where Liko's parents Davey and Michele had been married decades before. The couple had returned from Hawaii days earlier than expected to bury their only son; even so, Davey's brother, Michael Kenney, did not feel a sense of urgency on their part. "It took a while for them to get their plane tickets," Michael recalls. "I jumped on the phone to Davey and told him that he really needed to get back here. If it was my kid, I would have been on the next plane to New Hampshire." Liko's sister Mahina had also returned, no doubt saddened and trying to come to terms with her turbulent relationship with her brother. Liko's uncles and aunts were also in attendance. One noted absence was his celebrated cousin Bode Miller. Some questioned how the ski champion could brush off such an occasion, but those who knew Bode Miller knew better. Bode wasn't one for funerals. He hadn't even attended services for his beloved grandmother Peg Kenney a decade before and a year after Jack Kenney had finally succumbed, following a long battle with Alzheimer's disease. Bode had said goodbye to his grandmother in his heart and had spent the rest of that day skateboarding with his buddies. He probably had a similar response to the shooting death of his wayward cousin Liko.

The memorial service was open to the public but the Kenney-Miller family decided at the last minute to bar members of the media from attending. It is a rare event when such attention is paid to the funeral of a cop killer but this had been no ordinary police shooting from the very beginning. Unlike McKay's funeral, there were no bagpipes wailing at the Tamarack Tennis Camp. Instead, Liko's sister Mahina blew a spiraled conch shell as mourners watched her and her parents perform the Four Directions ceremony. The ritual, traditionally performed at Hawaiian weddings, is the placing of four stones in the direction of north, south, east, and west to invoke the elements and spirit of nature. The funeral had a Polynesian vibe but there was also a Native American influence to the whole affair. Many in attendance burned sage sticks in a tradition called smudging: participants light the end of a stick and let it burn for ten to fifteen seconds before blowing out the flame and directing the smoke around their bodies to ward off nefarious forces.

Family friend Bill Briggs spoke first: "We are gathered here to celebrate what is good, what is true and what is beautiful in Liko's life." Briggs looked out over the crowd and beyond to the rain-soaked field around them. "You bring today an enormous amount of grief. The rain that we hear and feel and see around us are God's tears on this day. Today we are going to talk about love and we are going to feel love around us." Mourners let the words soak in as they stared down at Liko's picture on the cover of his memorial program. The photo showed a happy, yet defiant, young man with eyes closed and a clenched fist raised high in the air.

Liko's parents also shared their memories of their long-haired boy and spoke of his dream to move to Oregon to raise cattle.

They had done their best to put on a brave face for the crowd. "Davey always said he doubted if his son would reach term [adulthood]," Mike Kenney says. It was also a time for many of Liko's relatives and friends to look inward and examine themselves. "We all asked ourselves, what could we have done?" Mike Kenney remembers. "Maybe Liko didn't get the right support from the folks around him."

Guilt also weighed on Franconia resident Kate Goldsborough, who told mourners that young people had approached her and expressed their fear and concerns about Bruce McKay. "We have a job to do here. We need to band together. If we ever have a situation go on again, something that is not right, people must band together, as scary as that might be and all of us have to stand up. We have to do something to change it. I wish we had all banded together and stood up for what was right for Liko."

Another family friend, spiritualist Paula Wolcott, then led the group in prayer. "Liko was a good-hearted albeit spirited young man coming into his own. Because of a clash of differences, his life here ended in a sudden tragic loss of life, leaving us bewildered and heartbroken." The gatherers then harmonized to K. D. Lang's ballad "Simple" from her album *Hymns of the 49th Parallel*, which includes the lines:

Flawless light in a darkening air
Alone . . . and shining there . . .

12

The real news is bad news.
MARSHALL MCLUHAN

Soon after the contingent of police officers departed Franconia Notch, the paradigm of public sentiment began to shift away from Bruce McKay to his killer. On May 19, 2007, the *Concord Monitor* covered a wreath-laying to remember all forty-two New Hampshire law enforcement officers killed in the line of duty, including Corporal McKay. The next day the newspaper ran a column titled "Even in tragedy, we must ask." It was in response to a previous editorial that had called for the police video capturing McKay's death to be released to the public. Many readers had voiced their outrage about such a request, but the *Monitor* editorial board maintained that a full profile of Bruce McKay could not be written until their staff had a better handle of the events that led up to the shooting. "Our reporters are not plugged in to Franconia the way they are plugged in to the Concord area," *Monitor* columnist Mike Pride wrote. "Some people who spoke with our reporters echoed a letter writer from Franconia who portrayed McKay as 'an upstanding police officer' who looked out for local kids. Others had troubling things to say about his record. Because they would not allow their names to be used, we could not publish what they had to say. No person in a public role is without detractors, but we were not certain we could do a fair, balanced, truthful story on McKay's life and record. So we passed." Like many in the media, Mike Pride had begun to question the initial theme of "two heroes and one villain." The columnist also criticized New Hampshire law enforcement officials for not offering a detailed narrative of the events of May 11, 2007. Pride went out of his way to praise Attorney General

Kelly Ayotte but did question why she felt the need to exonerate Greg Floyd so quickly.

The *Monitor*'s stance was daring, considering the political climate at the time. New Hampshire had buried two officers gunned down in the line of duty in the past seven months. No one had questioned Manchester police officer Michael Briggs's actions on the night he was killed, so why cast doubt on the actions of Bruce McKay? Those still grieving the Franconia police officer lashed out at the newspaper. Concord residents Brian and Jean Chase submitted a response to the *Monitor* that said in part, "This was the case of a trained police officer, attempting to serve and uphold the law as sworn, who was the victim of deadly force. Shame on you!" The Chases vowed to cancel their subscription immediately. Another reader, Brian Mayette of Cornish, New Hampshire, applauded the *Monitor*'s position: "I agree 100 percent with your coverage of the shootings in Franconia. . . . It's a shame you're getting so much flak for it. You are completely right on the mark." Mayette added: "You were right in avoiding blindly writing a laudatory profile of Corporal Bruce McKay when there are unresolved questions about his actions." The *Monitor*'s rival newspaper, the *Union Leader*, was a bit slower to take the angle that Corporal Bruce McKay may not have been the hero he had been made out to be. It was as if the ghost of right-wing publisher William Loeb was sitting in on the editorial meetings.

The people of Franconia didn't need the media to tell them how to feel; the entire community suffered post-traumatic stress in the weeks following the tragedy. In an unprecedented move for such a small town, officials created a volunteer outreach program to help with the healing process. Led by State Representative Martha McLeod, the Franconia Recovery Team was organized to "promote truth, healing and reconciliation" for local residents. McLeod also said the team's goal was to provide a clearinghouse for information, ideas, and rumors (a new one seemed to sprout out of the Franconia soil each day). Everyone appeared to be bracing for the release of the dash-cam video from Bruce McKay's police cruiser. Local newspapers and television stations had made their Right to Know requests to the attorney general's office and now the ball was in Kelly Ayotte's court.

The videotape was finally released to the public in late June 2007. It was supposed to be the final chapter of this "closed case"; instead, it sparked a firestorm of controversy, the flames of which are still burning today. The gaggle of media gathered in Concord, where the video, in the form of a DVD, would be handed out to those news outlets that had requested it in writing. As senior writer for WBZ-4 News in Boston, I had been assigned to the story that evening. My duty was to write the anchor lead-in to the reporter live shot and then manage the logistics of getting the "package" (report) on live television. In midafternoon, I had received a phone call that our photographer was ready to feed in the Franconia dash-cam video via satellite. I was anxiously standing by in ENG Receive, the electronic portal for all of our incoming and outgoing video.

The first image I saw was the view out of the windshield of Corporal McKay's police cruiser, which still showed the traces of a late afternoon downpour. McKay made no attempt to wipe away the scattered raindrops as he maneuvered his vehicle out onto Route 116. At first, it looked like nothing more than a leisurely drive in the countryside. McKay's vehicle did not appear to be traveling at a high rate of speed. I watched patiently as his cruiser bore right at Big Corner and then continued on straight until Liko Kenney's Celica came into view ahead in the distance. At this moment, McKay drove much faster, as Liko's car grew bigger and bigger on the small television screen. I watched the officer follow Kenney into a turnabout dominated by tall, gangly birch trees. Both vehicles stopped and I assumed Bruce McKay had then stepped out of the vehicle. Because his cruiser was parked at a slight angle, at no time during this initial stop did I see or hear Bruce McKay. While the video camera mounted on the windshield near the rearview mirror was activated automatically, the audio transmitter located on McKay's duty belt was not. The officer had to turn it on manually; from what I could hear, there was only silence. I could see Liko Kenney pop his head out of the window briefly before rolling it up. There looked to be some debate going on inside the vehicle between the driver and his passenger, Caleb Macaulay. The Celica idled for just more than two minutes before it suddenly lurched forward, kicking up dirt as Liko fled the scene. Liko turned right onto Route 116/Easton Road and was followed by McKay approximately ten seconds later.

ENG Receive is normally a beehive of activity during this part of the day, when video feeds begin coming in at a steady clip. Usually the technicians and writers are focused solely on the stories they are responsible for; on this day, however, everyone's attention had turned to the small screen carrying the dash-cam video. I had a sinking feeling in my stomach as I watched McKay pursue Kenney down a sun-splashed stretch of Route 116, which to me looked like a quintessential country road, dotted by small farmhouses surrounded by large open fields. McKay's cruiser gained ground quickly but remained about ten to fifteen feet behind the Celica. The vehicles kept at this pace for several more seconds until I could see McKay's vehicle pick up speed and pass Liko Kenney on the left. The officer then made what looked to be an awkward four-point turn before coming nose to nose with the Celica. Liko then pointed his left hand out the driver's-side window and signaled that he wanted to drive on to Tamarack. While part of me focused on this exchange between Kenney and McKay, I couldn't help noticing another vehicle come into view at the top righthand side of the screen. I knew right away that it was Greg Floyd's truck.

At this stage in the case, it was still unclear to journalists and the public as to what time Floyd had come across the scene. I had previously believed that he had arrived just before Bruce McKay was shot, but the videotape now told me something different. Floyd entered the fray just as McKay and Liko were squared off on Route 116. Still, this looked like nothing more than a routine traffic stop. Had Floyd been in any rush to get home, he could simply have passed both vehicles on the lefthand side and continued on. Instead he chose to pull off to the side of the road, becoming an active witness to what was about to unfold. My attention was drawn back to Liko Kenney, who appeared ready to give up the fight as he turned back into the gravel parking area. There were now only two objects in view, the hood of McKay's police cruiser and Greg Floyd's truck. Both vehicles were facing one another. I thought McKay would pull in immediately after Liko in an effort to block him from making a second escape attempt, but McKay waited seven full seconds before making his turn. The delay struck me as odd, but then I surmised that the officer could have been trying to determine whether Greg Floyd was a friend or foe. While the ex-Marine and his teenage son sat watching from their truck, McKay backed up slightly and then charged in after Liko Kenney. The young man immediately drove forward, possibly to attempt an escape or to avoid getting hit by McKay's cruiser. The officer reacted instantly by ramming his large SUV into the front grill of the much smaller Celica. The sheer violence of the collision stunned all of those watching it. I could hear a chorus of groans echoing from one end of ENG Receive to the other as McKay rammed Liko's car once more, pushing it back toward some old farm equipment. Liko had both hands up off the steering wheel now, clearly frightened by what was happening. Seconds later, Corporal Bruce McKay could be seen on the dash-cam video for the very first time as he strode swiftly toward Liko's window, his right arm outstretched holding a small canister of OC spray.

At this point in the video, McKay must have activated the audio transmitter on his duty belt because the silence had been immediately broken by the wail of a police siren. Corporal McKay made no more attempts to reason with Liko Kenney; instead, he doused him and his passenger with what looked to be the entire canister of pepper spray. My colleagues and I let out another collective groan as we watched Liko's head disappear under the orange fog.

None of us had time to catch our breath; a split second later, a gun appeared almost magically in Liko Kenney's hands. I heard one loud crack and then another and another as the weapon jerked in Liko's grip. The sound of gunfire was then replaced by the moans of a dying man as McKay slipped from view while trying desperately to make it across Route 116.

The cliché held true: you could have heard a pin drop. A room full of men and women, well accustomed to seeing terrible things, was totally silent. I looked around at my colleagues, trying to gauge their reaction to what we all had just seen. Not one of us could come up with words to describe it; the sentiment, however, could be seen on all our faces. We were all shocked by what we had just witnessed and equally appalled by the actions of Liko Kenney and Bruce McKay. The video feed ended with Liko Kenney driving away from the view of the dash-cam recorder. We had been spared the images of the young man running down the officer with his vehicle. We also never got to see or hear Greg Floyd's deadly confrontation with Liko. There were still many questions to be answered in this case, but it became much clearer that the officer's actions were overaggressive and had certainly contributed to his own death.

The video was aired by television news outlets across the country and later uploaded onto YouTube. The popular Web site was successful at blocking most of the comments from its viewers but the Webmaster did allow some to get through. One user with the crude webhandle *Busterhymenout* wrote an equally crude comment after viewing the video: "That's what he [McKay] gets for being a dick and thinking he was above the law fuck that punk ass cop." Another YouTube user with the webhandle *djelement563* was a bit softer in his or her statement but the sentiment was the same: "From the looks of the video clearly the officer has an abusive authority problem, . . . That cop just messed around with the wrong people." Bruce McKay did have some supporters on the site. *MFFare1985* wrote: "Good that the SOB [Liko] got what he deserved. Not only did he shoot a policeman, but the asshole drives over him also?" Most of those who did come to McKay's defense were also quick to point out the officer's apparent lack of judgment on May 11, 2007. "Very sad that this officer let an ongoing pissing match escalate to his death," *mrwool983455* wrote. "Only a rookie would turn there [*sic*] back like that after unnessisarily [*sic*] macing someone. Sad for driver and cop that he didn't just wait for backup."

It is one thing to be questioned by elements of the lunatic fringe roaming cyberspace; it is quite another to be questioned by one of your comrades. Marc Lidsky is a decorated veteran of the Rhode Island State Police; he has patrolled highways there for nearly twenty years and has conducted more than a thousand police stops. I asked him to analyze the videos of both the 2003 incident and the final showdown of 2007. "In police work there is going to be the perception from an officer's view and there is the perception from the public," Trooper Lidsky explains. "It's hard to see eye to eye with both and it seldom does. In this case, reviewing the 1-26-03 stop, Corporal McKay is investigating a suspicious vehicle. He is calm towards Kenney and does not raise his voice and acts in a professional manner. Kenney is obviously not compliant and attempts to flee the scene; however, he is blocked by the cruiser. Corporal McKay did the right thing calling for backup and did not engage the situation until other officers arrived. If you get stopped by an officer, never exit the vehicle unless requested by the officer. When Kenney exited the vehicle without the request of an officer this can be taken as threatening behavior from an officer's safety standpoint. As for shining the cruiser's light in Kenney's direction, Corporal McKay more than likely did not want to illuminate himself in the car as a target after he directed him back to his car, which Kenney failed to comply. If Kenney complied with the officers as well as Corporal McKay, I believe it would not have escalated to the level it did. All of the officers showed restraint in this dealing with Kenney."

Lidsky does believe Bruce McKay made some fatal mistakes on
May 11, 2007. "With the knowledge at hand from a police report
that a subject [Liko] may be in possession of a gun, and you know
the vehicle is being operated by that subject, you don't have to
stop that vehicle right away," he says. "Notify dispatch that you
are following the vehicle waiting for another officer to initiate the
stop. If there is a threat of a handgun in the vehicle after the vehicle is stopped, you're obligated to conduct a felony car stop where
your weapon is drawn, the cruiser is positioned behind the suspect
vehicle, and all of your instructions are broadcasted via the police
loudspeaker not leaving the protection of your cruiser. Also the
other officer if available is also drawing down on the threat. As for
the traffic on the road during the pursuit it appeared to be light
and on a rural road. It was not a heavily populated area. As always
there is a threat to the safety of the public during any pursuit; however, it is much less than if it was a densely populated area. When I
viewed Corporal McKay's cruiser pushing Kenney's car backwards,
I would not have exposed myself to a potential threat, because
once again there might be a handgun in the car. If it was a drunk
driver and you had an idea that there was no weapon in the car this
is a technique I may have used. At the time of Kenney's car coming to a complete stop this is when a felony car stop should be used
with the information at hand. After deploying the pepper spray
I would not have turned my back. As it unfolded the way it did,
from the pepper spray I would have gone right to the duty weapon
verbally commanding Kenney 'Let me see your hands! Get out of
the car. Down on the ground!' From there I would take control of
the scene as well as securing any passengers in the vehicle."

Unlike most civilians who watched the May 11, 2007, video,
Trooper Lidsky does *not* believe McKay used excessive force. "Corporal McKay obviously wanted to use the least amount of force to
effect the arrest. This is evident due to the fact there was no signs
of a physical engagement, baton, tazer, etc. The effects of pepper
spray are only temporary. It certainly appeared Corporal McKay

did not want any bodily harm done to Kenney. Once again, you never know how you will act during any high-stress situation, but your training and experience helps you get through it. This was a very unfortunate incident for both parties where ultimately they both lost their lives."

After reviewing both videos countless times, I share Trooper Lidsky's assessment of the 2003 police stop: Officer Bruce McKay showed tremendous restraint during his encounter with a belligerent Liko Kenney. I thought back to my own youth, growing up on Cape Cod, dealing with a small-town police force bent on breaking up keg parties and other teenage gatherings. Had I questioned the authority of those officers I probably would have received much harsher treatment than Liko Kenney did. This encounter also strongly influenced Officer McKay's actions the next time around. McKay knew there was little chance of a rational response from Liko Kenney. The 2003 incident must have been playing out in McKay's mind when he reached for the pepper spray in 2007. He had tried to reason with Liko on that frigid January night and was injured as a result. McKay was not going to let Liko dictate the terms of the police stop again. He reached for the canister of OC spray with the belief that he could contain Liko before the young man got out of his Toyota Celica (as he had in 2003). Yet this strategy was fatally flawed, especially as McKay knew and had warned others that Liko carried a gun. Why the officer had not ordered Liko to keep both hands on the steering wheel while he conducted a search of the interior of the car remains a mystery. An even bigger question is, Why had McKay put his life in jeopardy over something as insignificant as an expired registration sticker?

❧ One month after authorities released videos of both the 2003 encounter between Liko Kenney and Bruce McKay and the deadly shooting of 2007, they disclosed the officer's use of force record to the public. McKay had filed twenty-four such reports over a ten-year period between 1997 and January 2007. He had written a report in 1997 after he had helped capture the two men who had murdered Epsom, New Hampshire, police officer Jeremy Charron. McKay had handcuffed Gordon Perry's accomplice Kevin Paul after Paul threatened him. Five more reports were filed the next year, including two where McKay had fired his service weapon to scare off bears. In 2005, McKay pepper-sprayed two students during a scuffle in the office of Profile High School. The officer had warned everyone ahead of time to clear the room before he used the OC spray; nonetheless, the toxic fumes got into the school's ventilation system, causing several students to get sick.

A year later, McKay pepper-sprayed and handcuffed an Ithaca College student for a suspended registration. The arrest was recorded on dash-cam video and would also find its way onto You-Tube. The incident occurred just after 8 P.M. on March 19, 2006. Corporal McKay had pulled Sarah Emberley over in the parking lot of the local supermarket, then known as Kelly's, for going 54 mph in a 30 mph zone. "Is there a reason for your speed?" McKay asked in a low, monotone voice. "Are you sure?" Sarah responded, still trying to comprehend why she had been pulled over. McKay then asked for her license and registration and told the driver to wait in the vehicle. He returned a few moments later with some bad news. "You're under suspension," McKay said. "You've been under suspension, I guess, for awhile."

"I'm sorry?"

"Your driver's license is under suspension," he informed her.

Emberley immediately protested, claiming that McKay's information was incorrect.

"Have you been drinking today?" he asked.

"No," she replied.

"Have you been drugging today?"

Again Sarah said no. McKay then ordered her to turn up her window and turn off her car. "You're in custody," he told her.

"Are you serious right now?" she asked, with a touch of panic in her voice.

"How many times do I have to say it?"

"You've only said it once so far."

McKay was clearly annoyed. "Well, I said it probably enough."

"Okay, I'm sorry, but you just said it once," she reminded him. "And for me that's a freak-out situation!" Emberley then began to cry. "I don't understand," she said, over and over again. "I have done everything legal my entire life."

McKay then asked the driver to button her pants, which were undone at the time. "I'm a ski racer and I had a friggin' ski race today and it's like a thousand degrees," she explained. At that moment, Sarah stepped out of her vehicle and walked around to the trunk of her car. "I'm training on fucking Monday," she muttered to herself. "This whole process is very upsetting for me because I do everything legal." Emberley then read off her résumé to McKay, informing him that she was a Big Sister in the Big Brother/Big Sister program and that she was also a successful ski coach. McKay listened patiently.

At this point, I wondered to myself why this video had been uploaded onto YouTube in the first place. In my estimation, the officer had not done anything to provoke or antagonize the woman. McKay may not have been willing to lend a sympathetic ear to her plight, but that was not in his job description. I was sure that nearly everyone McKay had pulled over during his career had offered some kind of excuse. As the driver attempted to retrieve a pair of shin guards from the trunk of her car, the encounter began to turn violent. "I'm training slalom on Tuesday and I'm coaching kids, that's my job," Sarah explained. "I need to take my shin guards; unfortunately, that's part of the deal."

"There is no deal," McKay told her angrily. "I write the rules. Put the shin guards back in the car."

At this point Sarah closed the trunk and took a step forward. McKay reached out and tried to grab her. "Don't touch me," she pleaded.

"You're under arrest," McKay said.

"No I'm not," Sarah replied, as she began to walk away. McKay followed and grabbed her by the back of the shoulders and pushed her up against the trunk of the Nissan Altima. "Don't fucking touch me!" she screamed. "Put your hands behind your back!" McKay barked. "Do you wanna get sprayed?"

The young woman attempted once more to walk away as the officer held both of her arms behind her back. "Let go of the purse," he demanded. McKay pulled her back and slammed her on the hood of his police cruiser. "Help me!" she pleaded to some passing motorists. "Help me, fuckers!"

McKay slammed her once more against the hood of the cruiser and took out his small canister of OC spray. Without warning, the officer sprayed the driver in the eyes as she fought to break free from his forceful grip. Sarah let out several loud wails as the painful irritant entered her eyes. "Put your hands behind your back!" McKay shouted once again. At this point, however, the woman was screaming at the top of her lungs in a full frenzy. Her screams were followed by several loud sobs. She begged for some water to douse her burning eyes. "Are you gonna sit still?" McKay asked over her screams, as if taking some amount of joy from the pain he had caused. "Are you gonna cooperate or not?"

The video was truly painful to watch. Why did McKay allow a simple request for shin guards to devolve into a violent struggle? It is a question asked by many of the 1,228 people who later witnessed it on YouTube. "This video makes me sick to my stomach," wrote *HoopsPrincess*. "The fear and pain in Sarah's voice is heartbreaking. Bruce McKay was nothing but a pathetic bully who had no business representing the law." A YouTube user with the handle *dbo799* used even stronger words to describe his feelings after watching the video: "Trouble just seemed to find this guy and his use of force is what got him killed later on. TOO BAD IT TOOK SO LONG!!! WHAT AN ASSHOLE!" But much like the video of the Liko Kenney–McKay shooting, some saw this particular police stop in a different light. "Once again I see McKay taking more time than others would, using less force than others would, giving the woman all the rope she needed to either chill the situation out or hang herself, which she chose to do," wrote *rattlunhum*.

Later it was learned that Bruce McKay had been warned about his demeanor by a fellow officer in the Franconia Police Department. In a letter to Police Chief Mark Montminy in July 2005, Sergeant Mark Taylor said he had urged McKay to be less confrontational because it had caused him problems in the past. "Based on my previous knowledge of Cpl. McKay's demeanor, this matter-of-fact attitude can come across as *hostile* and *confrontational*," Taylor wrote. The incidents with Liko Kenney and Sarah Emberley cemented the belief among many Franconians that Bruce McKay was on a terror campaign against local residents, using Gestapo-like tactics wherever and whenever he could. McKay's friends and colleagues didn't see it that way, however. Sugar Hill Fire Chief Allan Clark, who had attempted to save Bruce's life while he was trapped under Liko Kenney's Toyota Celica, does not believe the man had a personal vendetta against anyone. "Friend or foe, Bruce would pull you over if he thought you were breaking the law," Clark insists. "He didn't play favorites and you had to respect that."

A dissenter from Clark's view is Franconia resident Timothy Stephenson. Stephenson, the brother of Sam Stephenson, claimed that McKay had been harassing him since December 2003. Stephenson said McKay had also pulled him over in the parking lot of Kelly's Supermarket. "When he approached the window he told me that he pulled me over due to an unregistered trailer," Stephenson said in a statement. "The trailer was registered but had a different sticker on the license plate. I asked him [McKay] how he would know *that* and he told me that he could see it even though he was 200 feet away." Stephenson claimed that McKay then said, "I can't give you a ticket this time, Tim, but you'd better watch yourself!"

"Bruce, you're not supposed to be harassing me like this," Stephenson replied.

"Whatever," McKay shrugged. "At least I didn't cost you any money."

Timothy Stephenson said he approached Franconia Police Chief Mark Montminy a few days later and complained about McKay and that the chief said he'd look into it, but he never did. Stephenson was arrested for disorderly conduct on April 30, 2004, and later filed a lawsuit against McKay, claiming the officer had bullied him and had behaved in "an unprofessional manner." Stephenson said that shortly after he had been arrested, McKay began demanding personal and financial information that had nothing to do with the charge against him. He also accused McKay of threatening him. "I am going to do whatever I can to get rid of you," McKay allegedly told him. The small claims lawsuit was eventually dropped when both sides agreed not to pursue it further.

❧ Liko Kenney was not the only member of his clan to have a run-in with Bruce McKay. Liko's famous cousin, Bode Miller, faced off in court in what *Sports Illustrated*'s Tim Layden called, "a scene right out of [the 1974 B-movie] *Macon County Line*." Layden had been writing a profile on Miller at the time and had accompanied the renegade ski champion to court to fight a speeding ticket he had been issued by Bruce McKay. Bode Miller was young and rich and could easily have afforded to pay the $500 fine. Before the hearing, McKay approached Miller and his agent Ken Sowles outside the courtroom. "It's on videotape and radar, son," the officer told Miller. "Just pay the fine and get on with your life." McKay then turned to Sowles. "This is a waste of his time and a waste of my time," he said. Bruce McKay was not only the officer who had issued the ticket; he would also act as the prosecutor in the case. Once the proceeding got under way, McKay presented videotape evidence that showed Miller had been driving at 83 mph at the time he was pulled over. When it was time to take the witness stand, Bode Miller told the judge that he had come to court "to try to get my fine reduced and to antagonize McKay. Officer

BAD BLOOD   \ 177

McKay has a vendetta against me." Corporal McKay denied this when he was questioned under oath. No telling whom the judge believed, but he did reduce Miller's fine from $500 to $250 without explanation.

As Bruce McKay's critics continued to paint a portrait of him as a rogue cop, citing instance after instance where they felt he went over the line, supporters of the officer fought once again to be heard. Alan Chan Dronnait of Bow, New Hampshire, wrote a letter to the editor of the *Concord Monitor* after the newspaper printed a partial list of complaints against McKay. "Picking on a dead man seems to be easy for the *Monitor*," Dronnait wrote. "I don't know if Cpl. McKay was aggressive or not as an officer, but I do know he didn't deserve four shots in the back and to be run over by a car. He doesn't deserve to be exploited on the front page of the *Monitor* in order to sell papers either."

13

> *Reconciliation should be accompanied*
> *by justice, otherwise it will not last.*
> CORAZÓN AQUINO

It is a colossal task to repair the wounds of a fractured community, but the men and women of Franconia saw it as a challenge that had to be met if the town were to have any hope of moving forward. After reading the concerns of some 140 residents who responded to a survey sent to townspeople in Franconia, Sugar Hill, and Easton, the Franconia Area Recovery and Reconciliation Committee issued its first report to the Franconia Select Board in July 2007. In its summary, the committee was careful not to choose one side over the other and recognized the failings of both Liko Kenney and Bruce McKay. "On the one hand, no one is condoning murder," the report stated. "However, there is a sense that it could have been prevented if either Liko Kenney had more respect for the law, or Bruce McKay had more skill at conflict management. . . . Although several people recommended doing nothing since 'time heals,' and it was 'time to move forward,' most comments reflected a mood that requires action in order to reduce the unsettled community mood."

Committee members said the questions residents believed needed to be addressed most had to do with the attitudes of both police officers and young people in the community. The public wanted its police officers to promote a climate of safety, not fear. By the same token, parents and community leaders had to do a better job of teaching kids to respect the work police officers do. Before making its recommendations to the Select Board, committee members had to recognize that the local government had already been painted into a corner about what it could and could not do. The Select Board could not expose itself to increased liability, especially as Liko's parents, Davey and Michele, had now hired an attorney to begin building a case for a lawsuit against the town. The Franconia Area Recovery and Reconciliation Committee kept its recommendations centered on three core issues. The group wanted a reevaluation of the Franconia Police Department's hiring, training, and accountability practices. It also called for regular meetings between townsfolk and police officers to discuss their concerns openly and to have a clear understanding of one another. Finally, the committee wanted more focus put on youth services in hopes of preventing problems between kids and cops from reaching another boiling point. Echoing the sentiment of Kate Goldsborough, who said she "wished" the community had stood up for what was right, one committee member said the tragedy was not simply a result of bad decisions made by two and possibly three men; instead, it was triggered by the community as a whole. "We talked about this as a community problem, not as a youth or police problem," Steve Heath, owner of the Franconia Village Store, told the Select Board. "We felt a sense of guilt among the group. We felt that as a community we had somehow failed, and we decided that we never wanted this to happen again." Board members listened intently as the group presented its three-page document outlining its recommendations. "The fact that it [the report] did emerge from within the community strengthens my belief in vox populi, the voice of the people," said Selectman Chairman Carl Belz. "So it comes to us from people who elected us."

As the committee presented its case to the Franconia Select Board, relatives and friends of Liko Kenney gathered outside the town hall but refused to go in. Instead, they sat on the town hall steps, many of them clutching a photo of the rebellious young man. One of those who felt his presence, if not his words, needed to be known was Caleb Macaulay, Liko's passenger. Macaulay, now two months removed from the most jarring event of his young life, had refused to speak to reporters that day. Much of the talk inside town hall had been about "moving forward," but how could Caleb move forward after watching his friend murder a police officer and then get killed in a flurry of blood and bullets right beside him? Macaulay knew his only hope for psychological healing lay somewhere beyond the towering mountains of Franconia Notch. At summer's end Caleb joined Liko's parents Davey and Michele on their coffee farm in Hawaii where he lived in an old VW bus that his friend had once called home.

As the seasons changed and the leaves turned from green to a robust collection of orange, red and yellow hues, the majority of Franconians did their best to put the tragedy in the rearview mirror of their lives. Conversation turned from the Liko Kenney–McKay case to the promise of the upcoming ski season; forecasters predicted a snow-filled winter and, for once at least, the prognosticators were correct. December and January had broken snowfall records in New Hampshire and the season as a whole would be the snowiest in 135 years. The cheerfulness soon evaporated, however; in early January 2008, a bill was presented to the state legislature calling for a portion of the Franconia Parkway to be renamed in honor of slain police officer Bruce McKay. The bill's sponsor was State Representative Martha McLeod, who also happened to be a member of the Franconia Area Recovery and Reconciliation Committee. The idea had been conceived by the officer's family, including his fiancée Sharon Davis, who had legally changed her last name to Davis-McKay. House Bill 1428 called for the portion of the Franconia Notch Parkway between mile markers 108 and 110 to be named in honor of Corporal Bruce McKay. The bill stated: "Corporal McKay was committed to his job as a law enforcement officer and prosecutor for the town of Franconia. While on duty, Corporal McKay patrolled the areas designated. He loved the area, and enjoyed hiking, fishing, swimming, picnicking, and photographing the area, especially Echo and Profile Lakes and the White Mountains." The bill also called for the appropriate signage to identify the tribute and movement on the project sixty days after the bill's passage.

Similar requests to honor fallen law enforcement officials had received overwhelming approval from state lawmakers and those they served. Manchester police officer Michael Briggs had been memorialized a year before when a section of U.S. Route 4 from the Northwood-Epsom town line to the Chichester-Epsom town line was renamed the Michael Briggs Highway. Fallen officer Jeremy Charron also had a traffic circle renamed in his honor in Epsom. The people of Epsom had every right to be proud of Charron, who had served on the town's police force and Briggs, who had grown up there. Many in Franconia, however, were less inclined to view Corporal Bruce McKay as a fallen hero worthy of their praise. Their collective outrage was voiced in a petition that had begun to circulate around town and that read in part: "We, the undersigned residents of Franconia, wish to make known that we are not in favor of H.B [House Bill] 1428. There are other people who have contributed to this community over the years that deserve this honor more than Officer McKay."

Representative McLeod urged her Franconia area constituents who either supported or opposed the legislation to attend an upcoming public hearing on the matter. One woman who had helped circulate the petition saw the hearing as a storm cloud on the horizon. "This is bad," Mickey De Rham told the *Caledonian-Record*. "Because there is already a division in the town over this whole thing anyway, and now this just digs it up again. It's totally inappropriate in my opinion to be naming the Notch highway after an individual anyway. . . . This is just opening old wounds and the town will never get over it if it happens." Other residents, including a fellow member of the Franconia Area Recovery and Reconciliation Committee, accused Martha McLeod of keeping the community in the dark about plans to memorialize the controversial police officer.

Passionate people on both sides of the heated issue met in a crowded room inside the Legislative Office Building in Concord, New Hampshire, on January 10, 2008. Support for the bill was spearheaded by Sharon Davis-McKay, who felt that she owed it to Bruce to attend. "(Bruce) was killed in an untimely and brutal murder," Sharon told lawmakers. "He should be remembered as a father and protector of community life." The Kenney family was represented at the hearing by Liko's aunt and Michael Kenney's wife, Beth Towle Kenney, who called the bill "a stab in the back" of the community and that it would not "encourage healing." Kenney had support from several community members, including an Easton selectman who felt that Representative McLeod had kept his little town "out of the loop." Republican Gregory Sorg, Easton's state representative, went as far to say that McKay's actions led to his own death and that an honor of any kind would "debase the currency of police heroism in the state." Reconciliation chairwoman Dr. Virginia Jeffryes urged that the controversial bill be put aside for at least a full year so that the community could continue in the healing process. Setting such a timetable angered one lawmaker in favor of the memorial. "What is too soon?" asked State Representative Alfred Baldasaro of Londonderry. "I'm not a psychiatrist. Ask his daughter [Courtney] that, 'When is it too soon?'"

State Representative Martha McLeod said incredulously that she "had no idea the bill would be so divisive." This curious comment instigated a scathing response from the editorial staff of the *Union Leader*. In an editorial printed on January 13, 2008, the *Union Leader* stated: "She says she had no idea it would be so divisive. As an elected official from Franconia, how in the world could she not know that? McLeod ought to withdraw the bill and let Franconia, not the Legislature, decide what kind of memorial it wants McKay to have. That is the only way to honor McKay while allowing the community to heal." The renewed controversy over his son's actions prompted Bruce McKay, Sr., to write his own letter to the people of New Hampshire, which was also published in the *Union Leader*: "I don't understand this argument on any level. I understand the heartache that the Kenneys feel at the loss of their son, Liko. God knows, I have that same feeling. Waste is waste, and the loss of a child is nearly unbearable regardless of the circumstances. There is good and bad in all we see, but there are not too many places where the good and the bad are so clearly defined. The attempt to honor my son by naming a portion of I-93 in Franconia Notch for him is an attempt on the part of the citizenry to acknowledge the men and women who put themselves in harm's way, the quick responders of all fields who each day put their uniform on and venture forth to attempt to control the sometimes hostile environment in which we live."

In late January 2008, the House voted 257-95 to shelve Bill 1424 for further study until 2009, when it was debated again, this time in the state Senate. Representative Martha McLeod reminded her colleagues that her bill had been unanimously supported by Franconia's Select Board. The decision by the House mirrored that of the state's Public Works and Highways Committee (the legislative body responsible for highway memorials), which voted 15-0 to delay the bill for one year because of division within the community. "We're doing what we've done for the last twenty-five years," said committee chairwoman Candace Bouchard of Concord. "[We are] giving time for that local community and its citizens to decide how they best want to honor their fallen officer . . . they have spoken out loud and clear." New Hampshire Attorney General Kelly Ayotte was on hand for the House debate and was disheartened by the vote, calling it "the wrong message to law enforcement."

Bruce McKay, Sr., was also disappointed by the apparent slap in the face to his son's memory. "If you tell the lie often enough, people will eventually believe it," he told the *Union Leader*. Later, he expressed to me some resentment against the people of New Hampshire—and Franconia in particular. "I never understood why Bruce was drawn to that place. There's a sort of outlaw mentality up there in the North Country and guns are a big part of that culture. I never understood why Bruce felt it was *his* job to protect *those* people."

❦ Bruce McKay, Sr., was just one of the living victims of the Franconia tragedy. I felt I had an understanding of what he and members of the Kenney clan were going through because I had experienced loss in my own family. My nineteen-year-old aunt Mary Sullivan was murdered in 1964 and was believed to be the youngest and last victim of the notorious Boston Strangler. As a journalist, I led a high-profile reinvestigation of the Strangler murders because my mother, Diane Dodd, had a sister's intuition that Mary's killer had never been found. What I discovered was that self-confessed killer Albert DeSalvo was not the Boston Strangler and that several men had committed these murders under the guise of a Jack the Ripper–type killer, stalking the women of Boston. In fact, police had strong suspects in at least six of the eleven Strangler murders, including that of my aunt. This man vanished in the months after her killing and I found him living in New Hampshire's North Country decades later. I eventually traveled north and confronted him with the evidence I believed had proved his guilt in the case. The stunned man offered me an alibi: he claimed he had been watching a football game on television on the day and time Mary Sullivan was killed. "You are an evil man," I told him. "I promised to find Mary's killer, and I may have, regardless of the fact that you'll probably never be prosecuted. I know you did it." I left the North Country with the feeling that I would one day return to see Mary's killer carted away in handcuffs. Unfortunately, this has yet to happen. Like all the Boston Strangler murders, the Mary Sullivan case remains open and officially unsolved.

I did return to the region several years later, but it had nothing to do with my aunt's murder. It had to do with the murder of a small-town police officer in the town of Franconia. I felt that this case, like that of the Boston Strangler, had so many questions yet to be answered. As a writer, I was drawn to the Franconia story because it was so universal. In every small town in America, one could find similar stories about the hard-nosed cop and the rebellious kid that could not get out of the other's way. But the question

I kept asking myself was, Why did the tensions between these two people spill over into murder?

It was a question that confounded me during the first of many trips to Franconia. I read several books on the area to prepare for my trip, including Floyd W. Ramsey's *Shrouded Memories*, a collection of unusual true-life tales about the history of the White Mountains. In it I came across another murder case that had rocked Franconia more than a century before. The killer was a scruffy-faced Englishman named Samuel Mills, and his photograph sent a chill up my spine. Mills had penetrating eyes that looked eerily similar to Liko Kenney's. I compared pictures of both men and let out a slight chuckle. Staring at the photographs, I was reminded of a line from the classic horror movie *The Shining*, in which Jack Nicholson's character is reminded that he had "always been the caretaker" of the haunted Overlook Hotel. However, unlike the Liko Kenney–McKay case, Samuel Mills was not forced by circumstance to take another man's life. He did it for the reason most crimes are committed: greed. Mills had been bunking at Obed Quimby's boardinghouse in Lisbon while working at the Dodge gold mine nearby. His pay from the mine was meager, so Mills decided to supplement his income by stealing a gold watch and about eighty dollars from a fellow miner. The theft was reported early the next morning, just as Mills had announced plans to travel to Landaff for the day. Samuel Mills had no intention of going to Landaff; instead, he walked nearly eleven miles to Franconia in the freezing rain to pay an unscheduled visit to George Maxwell's farmhouse on the Easton Road. Mills had learned that Maxwell recently sold property to a neighbor. The thief thought the farmer was now flush with cash and would be an easy mark. George Maxwell proved much less gullible than Mills had hoped when he opened the front door of his farmhouse some time after nightfall on December 8, 1866. "He [Maxwell] came and opened the door and I walked in," Mills said later. "He acted as though he was afraid of me. I said to him, "Don't you know me?"

The farmer did know the thief quite well. The two had often played cards in the kitchen of Maxwell's home. Something told him that Mills had not trudged through miles and miles of nasty winter weather for a simple game of cards. Maxwell picked up a stick of wood and held it up like a truncheon. "Get out of here!" he ordered Mills. At twenty-four, Sam Mills was much younger and much stronger than the elderly Maxwell. The thief attacked the farmer and threw him several times to the ground. Mills then grabbed a stick of wood and struck Maxwell as the man tried to escape to the pantry. *He's going to get his gun*, Mills thought as he gave chase immediately. At that moment, the candle that had illuminated the downstairs blew out and both men found themselves in the dark. Mills frantically fished for his jackknife and lunged forward, plunging the blade into the old man several times while Maxwell tried again to defend himself with sticks of wood. Mills grabbed some wood of his own and bludgeoned the farmer, who simply refused to give up. Mills could see Maxwell rise once again through the dim light shining from the wood stove. The thief reached for an axe and swung at the figure in the darkness. "And that finished him," Mills later told authorities. "He died hard."

Sam Mills rifled through Maxwell's belongings but could not find anything of value, so he had a cup of tea, stole the farmer's horse and wagon, and rode on into Franconia village. Like its owner, the horse was more stubborn than Mills had bargained for, so the killer abandoned the wagon and walked north to Littleton, covered in blood and leaving a distinctive track in the mud. Neighbors made the gruesome discovery of George Maxwell's body the next day. The farmer's head appeared to be badly bruised and the axe blade was still sticking out of his neck. By this time, Sam Mills had fled the area and stowed away on a freight train headed for Vermont. Mills made his way into Canada before heading back south to Detroit, Michigan, and then Chicago, Illinois. All the while, he pored over newspapers, looking for any articles about the grisly murder back in Franconia, New Hampshire. What Mills did not know was that a sketch of him was now being circulated in local newspapers and eventually nationwide. The drawing of a man fitting Mills's description found its way to Galena, Illinois, where police now had Mills in custody for an unrelated crime. The killer was returned to New Hampshire in February 1867 and put on trial two months later. Samuel Mills was found guilty and sentenced to hang. While awaiting his fate at the Old County Jail in Haverhill, New Hampshire, Mills did manage a successful but brief escape before being captured by a posse of men and led back to jail. After he was returned safely to custody, a new heavy chain was fastened to his ankle and secured to a beam in the center of his cell. Samuel Mills was hanged before a crowd of three thousand on May 6, 1868. Before taking his long, solitary walk to the gallows, the killer left a message on the wall of his jail cell: "Samma Mills murder, going to be 'ung today of May—good fellow but no man don't know it."

"Good fellow, but no man don't know it," I muttered to myself as I entered Franconia Notch behind the wheel of my black Volkswagen Jetta. It was now late winter; the snow piled high along the side of the highway was blackened by the exhaust fumes of the hundreds of vehicles that passed by each day. It was mud season in the North Country and my Jetta showed no visible signs of the car wash I had paid for just the day before. Also no longer visible were any signs of the area's most celebrated attraction, the Old Man of the Mountain. The profile was long gone, leaving only memories left in the minds of those who lived here. The same could be said of both Liko Kenney and Bruce McKay. Both were good men in their own way, *but no man don't know it*. I passed Cannon Mountain (where Liko's cousin Bode built his legend), while keeping an eye out for Exit 38 Franconia/Sugar Hill. Despite my complete lack of navigational skills, I made the exit and drove across the Route 18 intersection, over a bridge, and onto Route 116. *This is the road Liko took the night he was killed*, I thought as my stomach tightened. I slowed down my speed considerably as I approached a minefield of frost heaves that jutted out of the road like rippling sea swells. *How fast could Liko have been driving on a stretch of road like this?*

I now had both hands on the steering wheel as I hit each bump, wondering whether my little car could absorb such punishment. My thoughts quickly drifted back to Liko Kenney and Bruce McKay. I had studied the dash-cam video hundreds of times and now here I was, turning the Big Corner, following the same route that had ended in the deaths of both men. I felt locked in some kind of virtual reality game. This was reality, but it was no game. *What were Liko and McKay both thinking?* I tried to get inside their heads as I slowly approached the scene of the crime. During the pursuit, did McKay pause to remind himself about the warning he had given other officers—that Liko Kenney had a gun? Did the officer also realize that he was not wearing his protective vest? As for Liko Kenney, was his sole focus now getting to the Tamarack Tennis Camp, or had it shifted to the .45 Hi-Point that was loaded and resting near his feet? I spotted the dilapidated white barn on the right side of the road and knew I was close. I put my blinker on and turned slowly into the gravel area. I noticed that none of the farm equipment had been moved since the shooting. The scene looked exactly as it had on that fateful night in 2007. As I stepped out of my vehicle, I heard the distant echo of a thunder clap rolling off the nearby mountains. It had rained for much of the morning but beams of sunlight were beginning to peek through the darkened clouds. The sound of thunder showed the storm still had some energy left, and it startled me for a moment. The thunder was reminiscent of a gunshot; I stood waiting for several more to come but they did not. The skies grew quiet as I knelt down to rub some dirt between my fingers. Alone in this spot I had the same feeling I had once experienced while touring a Civil War battlefield. Something tragic had happened here. This too was sacred ground in its own way.

I made the sign of the cross and got back in my car. I drove across the street to the Kinsman Lodge, unpacked my belongings, and walked inside where I was greeted by innkeeper Sue Thompson. Thompson had short gray hair, a kind face, and a thin build, which she said was the result of her passion for skiing. I told Mrs. Thompson that I was a writer but did not reveal the subject I was working on at first. We had a pleasant chat about the bounty of snowfall for the season and the hope for a quiet spring. I then explained the nature of my visit and shared with her my concerns. "As a guy from Boston, I'm afraid folks here may view me as an outsider," I said. "They might be less willing to open up about their feelings surrounding the case." Mrs. Thompson looked at me as she folded her arms and began walking into the inn's breakfast room to a set of bay windows that provided a sweeping view of Route 116 and the crime scene. "A lot of people had problems with Bruce McKay," she told me. "Some say he had vendettas against certain people in the community. I don't know anything about that, but I will say that he certainly made his presence known. I used to see a police car go up past the inn to the Easton town line and turn around three times a day. Since the shooting I haven't seen one since."

Like many of those I had heard talk about the case, Sue Thompson called it a tragedy on both sides. She did say, however, that she was opposed to renaming a stretch of highway in the officer's honor. "Who are you going to talk with first?" she asked.

"I'm gonna try to interview Greg Floyd," I told her. "He appears to be the wild card in this whole thing."

The reflective yet pleasant look on her face was replaced by fear. "I'm worried for you," she said. "I went by Hummingbird Lane myself once but I wouldn't dare go any further."

I told her that I appreciated the concern but that I'd be okay. I had come face-to-face with suspected killers before in the Boston Strangler case and I dismissed it as "just part of the job." I grabbed my overnight bag and Thompson led me up a narrow flight of stairs to the second floor. "You're in Cannonball Three," she smiled while pointing down the long hallway. I walked along creaking wooden floorboards toward my tiny but well-decorated room, which consisted of a single bed, dresser, and a small lamp. The space was cozy, a little cramped, even, but I knew I wouldn't be spending much time here. I pulled out a couple of notepads and my tape recorder and went over the questions I had planned to ask Greg Floyd. Obviously, the contradictions he gave investigators regarding his military service were of great concern to me. Whether he would stick to that story or offer me the truth remained to be seen. Of greater concern was the dangerous mixture of prescription drugs he had taken on the day of the shooting. I was sure the bottles came with the usual warning: DO NOT OPERATE HEAVY MACHINERY. In Floyd's case, the warning should have read: DO NOT HANDLE A DEADLY WEAPON. How would he react when I told him that he had been a prime candidate for Serotonin Syndrome, which could have dangerously altered his judgment on the day of the shooting?

I had also planned to pin him down about the moments just before he pulled the trigger, killing Liko Kenney. Floyd had originally said that he offered no warning to Kenney. Caleb Macaulay also told investigators Floyd had not said a word before he opened fire. Why did Floyd change his story and tell authorities that he did order Kenney to put down the gun? I hoped the answers to the questions lay ahead at Hummingbird Lane. I returned to my car and drove south on Easton Road past the Tamarack Tennis Camp toward Floyd's home. Before I had left for the journey north, I told a colleague of mine at WBZ about my hope to interview Greg Floyd. "Are you crazy?" she asked. "The guy is disturbed and the area he lives in is quite remote." I came to realize how remote the area was as the charming farmhouses I had passed earlier were now few and far between. The terrain was now one of dense woods with trees so tall they nearly blocked out the sun. I felt truly alone. I had not seen another car pass me for miles. Was this the mean-

ing of the Joseph Conrad title "The Heart of Darkness?" I let out
a nervous laugh and turned up the volume of my CD player. Mick
Jagger wailed on about having some "Sympathy for the Devil"
and I thought, *how appropriate*. I finally reached Hummingbird
Lane and it looked like nothing I had imagined. It was a charming little dirt road, complete with a pretty white mailbox at the
head of the street. I turned in and turned down the volume of my
car stereo. "This isn't so bad," I whispered to myself. Hummingbird Lane was a winding one-way road and I was forced to drive
no faster than 10 mph; the surface was icy and I didn't know what
was ahead of me.

I approached a driveway that I knew led to Greg Floyd's home.
It was surrounded on both sides by cut logs and tall pines posted
with signs that read: STAY OUT—NO TRESPASSING FOR ANY
REASON. VIOLATORS WILL BE TOWED. "Or shot," I said to
myself. The brief moment of calmness I had felt was gone now.
Two Greg Floyd phrases kept running through my head: "My dog
is trained to attack the throat and the groin" and "Get the pouch!"
Would I get the same rude welcome that meter reader Shay Littlefield had received? Or was I in store for something worse? "Fuck
it," I said aloud. "I came all this way. I gotta hear what Floyd has
to say." I pulled my Volkswagen Jetta into the driveway and proceeded with caution. The driveway appeared about as long and
winding as the road had been and my heart began to beat faster as
I drew closer.

I made it about halfway down the driveway when I decided it
was time to back off. I wasn't a police officer. I didn't have a gun.
I was a journalist armed only with a notepad and a tape recorder.
The words "THROAT" and "GROIN" were echoing in my head
now. I could live with being called a coward; at least I'd live. I put
my foot on the brake pedal and shifted the car into reverse. The
Jetta moved backward but only for a moment. The back wheels
started to spin and I was going nowhere. "Shit, shit shit!" I said
aloud as I pulled forward and then tried backing up once again.

The wheels spun on the deep snow and ice but could not gain traction. I reached for my cell phone but I had no reception. The cell phone was dead. "The only way to get outta here is to go forward and turn around," I convinced myself. It certainly wasn't the option I had hoped for. I drove slowly down the driveway and briefly thought of the tagline from the movie *Alien*: "In space no one can hear you scream." *Well, in deep woods, no one can hear you scream either!* I turned down my window and hoped to hear some signal of life in the distance, a car coming down the road, a neighbor's voice in the distance. I heard nothing. I then realized that the silence could be a good thing. *Maybe Floyd's not home.* I pulled up to his log cabin and awkwardly attempted to turn the car around. *If he sees me I gotta at least explain myself.* I stepped out of the car and walked slowly to the front door of Greg Floyd's home and knocked. I waited for what felt like an eternity. In reality though, it was no more than fifteen seconds—just about the time it would take him to retrieve his arsenal from his bedroom. I strode swiftly back to my car and tore out of the driveway, skidding briefly on the ice before gaining control. I turned out onto Hummingbird Lane and kept one eye on the rearview mirror. I was convinced I'd see Floyd's truck appear behind me at any moment, ready to knock me off the road. I reached the main road and felt I had reached salvation.

On the drive back to Franconia I cursed myself for allowing my fears to get the better of me. Approaching Route 116, I noticed a figure standing by the side of the road in the distance. It looked like some kind of scarecrow. As I got closer, I realized it was an old woman and she was holding a handmade cardboard sign reading: FRANCONIA. The woman had on a floppy brown hat covering her straight, almost white hair. She wore a green parka and was holding a green backpack decorated by two large feathers. The woman looked like she'd stepped out of a *Harry Potter* novel, but she did not appear to be a threat. I was growing tired of yelling at myself so I decided to give her a lift into town. She called herself

Jeanne and offered no last name. "I'm goin' to the dump," she told me. "Gotta do my outdoor chores so that I can do my indoor chores this weekend." She muttered something about painting her house and not having access to a car. I mentioned that I had just come from the Floyd place. "See you still have your head," Jeanne observed. "That's a good sign. I could tell you a lot about Floyd, but we're all afraid." I told her that I was only trying to interview Floyd for a book I was writing about the case. This drew a hearty laugh from the old woman. "Everybody's writing a book," she said, with a wide smile lining her weathered face. "This is a very poor town and everyone wants their fifteen minutes of fame. Everyone wants their piece of the pie." I told her that I hated pie and that I only hoped to explain why this tragedy happened. "Greg Floyd's a major piece of the puzzle," I said. We pulled into the town dump a few minutes later. Jeanne got out of the car, thanked me for the ride, and offered some advice. "Stay away. You look like a nice fella. Floyd won't hesitate to blow your brains out."

I didn't curse myself after that. Maybe Jeanne knew something I didn't. I continued into town and stopped off at the Franconia Police Station. I tried to open the front door but it was locked. I peered inside and was taken aback at how small the office was. My dorm room in college had offered more space. I rang a buzzer, which got me connected to a dispatcher in a nearby town. "I'm sorry," I told her. "I thought this was the buzzer to be let inside." I returned to my car and saw a pleasantly dressed older woman walking her basset hound along the side of the road. Whereas "Jeanne" had looked the epitome of a frontierwoman, Kathy Mead was modern and chic. Neatly attired with clothes directly from the L.L. Bean catalog and well coiffed, Mead introduced herself and her dog Zeke with a friendly handshake. "My husband Bill is the retired fire chief," she told me. I asked Kathy Mead how she felt about the case and she echoed what Sue Thompson had told me. "The majority of people thought it was a tragedy on both sides," Kathy said. "Most folks went to both funerals. I didn't know Liko and I had only met McKay a few times. I guess it comes down to your personal experiences with either one." Mead said she first met Bruce McKay at a town meeting on appropriations for improvements to the tiny police headquarters. "Things got pretty heated," Mead recalls. "But Bruce was the voice of reason. He spoke very calmly and brought people together. He was a 'law and order' type and is one that some people liked while others didn't."

I thanked Kathy for her concise analysis and patted ol' Zeke on the head before heading back to my car. As I did so, a Franconia police vehicle pulled up alongside. Chief Mark Montminy introduced himself and welcomed me inside. The first thing I noticed as I stepped inside the small office was a small picture of Bruce McKay with a donation sign for a family fund. Chief Montminy was cordial but appeared to carry the stress of his small department squarely on his shoulders. He sat down behind his desk and asked me to wait while he listened to his phone messages. "I can't talk about case specifics due to pending litigation," he informed me, while running his fingers through his crew cut.

"Okay then, tell me about Bruce."

Montminy sat back in his chair, pulled on his gray mustache and waited for the right words to come. "I'll tell you about Bruce," he said. "He was a great father and was wrapped around Courtney's little finger. She's a brave little girl who's gonna have to read all about this someday." The words hit me like a baseball bat across the face. Montminy was right. One day Courtney may read the words I would write about her father. I certainly did not want to destroy the image she had of him, but I knew it was my job to paint an accurate picture of all the figures in this case—the good *and* the bad.

"What are your plans for the anniversary?"

"We'll go to the service down in Concord," Montminy told me. "Concord's the least we could do for Bruce." The chief then urged me to go to the town hall and see the portrait of Bruce and the painting Bruce's father had done in his memory. "It's called

Field of Dreams," the town hall clerk told me as we gazed at the large canvas covered by yellow and orange brush strokes. "It's the meadow in back of Bruce's house in Landaff." I complimented the painting and asked the clerk her thoughts about the case. "All this talk about Liko Kenney having special dispensation to have another officer at the scene is just crazy," she said. "You saw how small our police station is. One officer is on at a time, you get what you get!" The clerk then talked about the coordination that went into Bruce McKay's funeral. "The family wanted a full military-like funeral. Mourners had to be bused from location to location. Most folks just stayed home and watched it on TV. It was rainy and cold, but Bruce would have liked it that way. The weather was fitting for the occasion." I added a small donation to the Courtney McKay fund and left town hall thinking that I had only one side of the story. It was now time to get the other side.

My next stop was the Dutch Treat, Franconia's local restaurant and watering hole. It was only two thirty in the afternoon, but already the stools around the bar were filled to near capacity. I managed to find one stool at the end of the bar near the kitchen. I sat down and ordered a Sam Adams. I looked around at the five men huddled around the bar, all with facial hair of varying lengths. The hair on top of their heads was either tucked under a cap or combed neatly in a ponytail. Pabst Blue Ribbon was the beer of choice for them all. Like most bars, the interior was dark. One wall was covered with pictures of Bode Miller as well as old-time Red Sox players. A wall-mounted plasma screen TV near the opposite end of the bar was the only hint at twenty-first century convenience. The channel was set to GAC (Great American Country) and at this moment featured a music video by Toby Keith: "Country of Red, White & Blue." I sipped my beer and listened to the conversation at the bar. The young bartender was chatting with the regulars about Mardi Gras night at a biker bar.

"What's that biker club up Vermont?" one asked.

"The Mountain Men," someone replied.

"Yeah, they were all there with their girlfriends," the bartender noted. "Girls were handing out beads." This drew a loud whoop from the patrons.

"I know the Mountain Men," one guy chimed in. "They all lost their driver's licenses and I've seen 'em hitchhiking with their girlfriends on the side of the road." He let out a throaty laugh, grabbed his pack of GPC cigarettes off the bar and went outside for a smoke. The bartender pulled out a jar and waved it in front of me. "Fiddlehead to go with the beer?"

I had no idea what a fiddlehead was. It sounded to me like some sort of small crab. I didn't want to be impolite so I took one. "I pickled these myself," the bartender said proudly. "Garlic's the secret. I mix it with dill and vinegar." I sucked down the spicy fern leaves and asked for another. I then told everyone at the bar why I was there. At first, I was met with only silence. To a man, everyone just stared down at their beer. I noticed that one guy was nervously peeling the Pabst Blue Ribbon label off his bottle. *Shit, this is exactly what I had feared. No one wants to talk to me.* A few moments later, however, the silence was broken by an eruption of chatter. The great debate had begun and nearly everyone had an opinion—much to the dismay of the Grump, an older heavy-set man with a thick beard. He voiced his displeasure with me immediately. "You've got no story here," he said, jabbing his stubby index finger my way. "You've got three assholes and two of 'em are dead. End of story."

A woman with blonde hair, whom I took to be Grump's wife, touched my hand gently. "Liko was a good kid," she said. "He was living a good life." This comment made the Grump roll his eyes. "Good kid? Liko was a fucking brat!" he shouted. "I knew him since he was four years old, screaming all the time. His parents didn't raise him right. His parents didn't raise him at all. Fuck Liko! Fuck McKay and Fuck Floyd!"

"I just came from Floyd's place," I told them. This news was met with an uproar. The patrons began talking over themselves just to tell me to stay away. "He'll give you that third eye," one man says. "He wants to be left the fuck alone so I say let's leave him the fuck alone!"

One fellow sitting at the other end of the bar, who hadn't said a word until this point, decided it was now time to speak. "I live in back of Floyd," he told me. "Never met him. Don't want to know him."

The Grump butted in next. "See, what did I tell ya? You've got no story here. People should just let it go. Move on. I've seen dozens of reporters in this town and they were all prettier than you!" The Grump took one last swig of his beer, paid his bill, and walked out of the bar without saying another word. He had been right about one thing: no doubt all the reporters that had come to Franconia were "prettier" than me. But he was wrong when he claimed there wasn't a story here.

The bartender who called himself Danny agreed with me. "There is a story here. A big story that no one's telling." I leaned forward over the bar as Danny whispered, "McKay and Floyd were setting Liko up. Floyd says he didn't know McKay—Bullshit! They knew each other all right. McKay wanted to take Liko out, but he got taken out too."

This conspiracy theory was not new. I had heard similar allegations from people in town. Not one of them, however, could find a tangible connection between Bruce McKay and Greg Floyd. What many of them pointed to was the dash-cam video from May 11, 2007. The conspiracy theorists found something odd in the seven-second delay between the time Kenney backed his Toyota Celica and the time McKay pulled in after him. "During this time, McKay had his radio turned off so he could communicate with Floyd by cell phone," one person told me. I just nodded my head and didn't push the issue. After nearly a year of researching the case, I had not found anything to connect Bruce McKay with Greg Floyd. I believed that both men were strangers brought together by circumstance.

At this time I was approached by the waitress. "Want another beer?" she asked. I declined the offer. She leaned closer to me. "Wanna talk instead?" she whispered. I eagerly accepted and followed her to the restaurant section of the Dutch Treat, where the two of us were nearly all alone in the large room. "My name is Diana," she told me. "I live in the woods, though, not in a castle." As we talked over coffee, I learned that Diana Brown wasn't just a waitress, but a spiritual adviser to many in Franconia's hippie community. "This is our share of the bad vibe," she explained. "This was our wake-up call like 9/11 was our wake-up call. Be appreciative of what you have because it can be gone at any time. I knew Liko. Sure he was headstrong, but who isn't at that age? Bruce McKay rode all the young people in this town. Some say they couldn't live here because of him. A police officer is supposed to guide youth, not get them killed." Diana pointed toward the sky. "McKay's probably up there thinking, I should've done something differently. Storm clouds have been hovering over this town for the past year. I don't know when we'll see the sun again."

My head was spinning by the time I returned to the Kinsman Lodge that night. Franconia felt a little like David Lynch's *Twin Peaks* to me. It seemed that everyone I met was just a little *off*. I didn't see this as a bad thing; in fact, it added to the peculiar charm of the town. The next morning, I paid a visit to Bill Kenney's cabin on the grounds of the Tamarack Tennis Camp. He told me that he too believed his nephew had been set up for murder. Kenney also believed there was a "secret police force" patrolling the North Country, harassing hippies and forcing them to flee. "It's about the land, you see," he tells me as his blue eyes dart around the cabin like a nervous bird. "The land is expensive and we hippies aren't interested in building condos so the secret police are trying to scare us into turning it over." I could certainly see how Bill Kenney could have influenced Liko's distrust of law enforcement.

"I'd like to pay my respects to Liko," I said, changing the subject. "Where is the cemetery?"

Bill Kenney stretched his arms out wide. "You're looking at it."

He smiled as he recognized the confusion on my face. "Lemme grab my boots and we'll go see Liko." Kenney put on a pair of rubber knee boots and a brightly colored cap and ushered me outside. "Are you ready for a little hike?" he asked. I nodded and let him lead the way. Two inches of fresh snow had fallen the previous night and had now mixed with the mud. I felt as if I were slogging through quicksand as I followed Bill Kenney up the mountain in back of his home. There seemed to be no clear path as we pulled back branches and navigated our way around snow-covered trees. "How much further?" I asked, feeling a little winded. "Just up ahead," Kenney promised. The dense forest soon gave way to a small clearing. "Here's where we talk with Liko," his uncle said sadly. We both walked up to the gray headstone lying atop a blanket of white snow. "This is where Liko wanted to be," Bill Kenney told me. "He's one with nature up here."

I noticed another stone at the opposite end of the clearing. "That's my brother Bubba's grave," he said. "We're standing in the middle of the Kenney family plot." I reached down and ran my finger across the top of Liko's gravestone. "Liko Peter Kenney," I said aloud. "April 26, 1983, to May 11, 2007." I then noticed some kind of Polynesian phrase engraved on the bottom of the stone just above the snowline. "Me Ke Aloha Pau'ole. What does that mean?"

"It means, with never-ending love," Bill Kenney explained. "Liko didn't have much peace in life. I hope that maybe he can find it here."

14

Whatever is begun in anger ends in shame.
BENJAMIN FRANKLIN

Bill Kenney and I met again a few weeks later for the trial of Greg Willis Floyd. Floyd had been cleared of any wrongdoing in the shooting of Liko Kenney, but the volatile ex-Marine could not stay out of trouble for long. In December 2007, Floyd had been accused of threatening his neighbor Alma Jean Boisvert out on Hummingbird Lane. The sixty-three-year-old woman told police that she was leaving home when she encountered Floyd's truck coming in the opposite direction up the narrow road. Neither vehicle could proceed unless one of the drivers moved out of the way. In order for Boisvert to clear a path, she would have to back her Lincoln Town Car up a hill and around a corner on a surface of snow and ice. The elderly woman knew this was an impossible task for her to perform, so she got out of her vehicle and approached Floyd's truck. "Do you have reverse?" she asked Floyd's son Gregory who was behind the wheel. At that point the elder Floyd leaned over into the driver's seat. "Do *you*, bitch?"

Alma Jean Boisvert had tried to avoid her neighbor ever since she had accused Floyd of firing a wild shot into her log home several years before. She had been successful for the most part, but now here she was, face-to-face with a seething, immovable object. "You've never backed up for me in the past," Floyd yelled. "I have backed up for you. It's about time you backed up for me." Finally, Greg Floyd stared at Boisvert with narrow eyes and said the words she dreaded to hear: "Do you want me to pull a gun on you?"

"No," the woman replied, her voice quivering.

"Because I wouldn't miss either," he promised.

Extra security was added at the Littleton District Courthouse when Greg Floyd finally went on trial for criminal threatening on April 15, 2008, nearly one month prior to the first anniversary of the McKay–Liko Kenney shooting. Authorities knew they had a powder keg on their hands from the very beginning. Greg Floyd's temper had been put on display during a pretrial hearing weeks before: he had lashed out in open court, saying that he had proved he could kill and that he would become violent again if his rights were denied to him. On the day of the trial, I saw a docile Greg Floyd enter the courthouse with the use of a cane. He had lost a great deal of weight over the past year and he appeared weak and emaciated. I then recalled the previous court case with Shay Littlefield. That case had fallen apart because the meter reader could not positively identify Floyd in court—and his unsureness stemmed from the fact that the defendant was then using crutches. Was Greg Floyd attempting a similar strategy this time around? The ex-Marine was accompanied by his son Gregory, who wore an ill-fitting gray suit, and his wife, Michelle, who unlike her husband appeared to be in terrible pain as she walked into court. The Floyds sat on a wooden bench outside the courtroom as they waited for Greg's attorney, William Christie, to arrive. I figured this would be the only opportunity I would have to introduce myself. I approached the family slowly and was met by a menacing gaze from Greg Floyd. "Is it possible to talk?" I asked. Floyd did not respond. Instead he just kept staring at me. "We're not talking," Michelle Floyd said quietly. "We just want to be left alone."

I may have had mixed feelings about Greg Floyd, but I had only sympathy for his wife. I nodded my head and walked back toward the crowd of reporters who stood waiting to be let into the courtroom. I looked around for Bill Kenney but did not see him. I had given him a ride from Tamarack to Littleton earlier that morning. He was about to come face-to-face with Liko's killer for the first time and Kenney was nervous. "Drop me off here," he said as we entered the center of town. "I wanna walk to the courthouse myself." I was unsure whether he would make it there. "Maybe he's had second thoughts," I muttered to myself as I continued on. I found a parking space on the street and walked across to the courthouse where I spotted an African American man getting his picture taken next to a satellite van from WMUR television in Manchester. I presumed him to be the controversial blogger Chris King. King had attached himself to the Liko Kenney–McKay case like a pit bull to raw meat; he had many supporters and just as many critics. King was the founder of kingcast.net, which had long called for the removal of New Hampshire Attorney General Kelly Ayotte and the imprisonment of Greg Floyd. On his Web site, King describes himself as a "sushi eatin', clog wearin', lawyer/civil rights activist." As for his occupation, King calls himself a "Metaphysical Reductionist." He also calls himself a lawyer, although he's been suspended from practicing. King got into trouble in his native Ohio in 2002 for illegally audiotaping a landlord who had allegedly called a tenant "nigger lover." King says he has not had the money to pay his fines and get his law license reinstated. He later resurfaced in New Hampshire where his online critics labeled him a self-promoter who has exploited the Liko Kenney–McKay tragedy for his own benefit—sort of a Don King of the North Country. With his manic personality, thin frame, and bespectacled appearance, he looked to me more like the sitcom character Steven Urkel on speed. Whatever King's true motives, one cannot deny that he has had his share of success. King was responsible for uploading the Sarah Emberley arrest video onto YouTube and he also released many of the Liko Kenney–McKay case documents on his Web site. He has been spurned by many so-called legitimate reporters, but Chris King has been a tenacious advocate for the Kenney family and a major thorn in the side of New Hampshire law enforcement.

"This is the big day," King informed me while puffing nervously on a cigarette.

"We'll see," I replied as I climbed a flight of steps to the courthouse. Once inside the courtroom, I sat with other reporters behind the prosecution table. I looked across the room and was pleased to see that Bill Kenney had decided to show after all. Wearing a yellow dress shirt over a pair of tan work pants, Kenney sat two rows behind Greg Floyd. His presence was felt immediately. The ex-Marine's bald head turned in Kenney's direction and he gave Liko's uncle the same menacing stare he had given me. To his credit, Bill Kenney did not take the bait and tried to focus his attention elsewhere. When it appeared that Kenney wouldn't play his game, Greg Floyd shook his head and laughed as he turned back around to face the bench. There were several more Liko Kenney supporters in the courthouse, many getting their first look at the man who killed their friend. Liko's boss Don Merrill even made a brief appearance before heading back to his Agway store. Liko's supporters were an eclectic mix of professional detectives and amateur sleuths, led by pied piper Chris King. All had taken Kenney's case as their cause célèbre. "Floyd's finally being held accountable for something," one supporter told me. "I wish he were going on trial for Liko's murder." Many felt this would be the only time they would ever see Greg Floyd stand before a judge.

As the trial got under way, Floyd did his best to keep his cane in plain view of Judge John P. Cyr, who would make his ruling on the case from the bench. The first to testify was New Hampshire State Trooper Nathan Johnston, who had interviewed both Floyd and Boisvert after the incident on Hummingbird Lane. "When I met her [Boisvert], she was extremely upset," said Johnston. "She was shaking." Floyd's attorney, William Christie quickly pointed out that there was no mention of Boisvert's dire emotional state in Johnston's police report and that she had declined a state police escort back home that evening. Christie also told the judge that it was the Floyds who had initially telephoned police after the encounter, not Alma Jean Boisvert. Greg Floyd told Trooper Johnston that he never threatened the woman because "she wasn't worth the bullet." During the trooper's testimony, Greg Floyd sat with his arms folded while frenetically raising his eyebrows, licking his teeth, and smacking his gums.

The only period where Floyd seemed at ease during the four-and-a-half-hour trial was when his wife and son took the witness stand to testify on his behalf. Gregory Paul Floyd had recently been fired from his job as a cashier at the Littleton Wal-Mart over allegations he stole several hundred dollars from the cash register. His credibility was in question, yet the younger Floyd appeared to be everything his father was not. The son did not carry himself in a threatening way; indeed, he approached the stand timidly and spoke in a soft, almost feminine voice. The nineteen-year-old said he was driving his father home from a trip to the doctor's office when they encountered Alma Jean Boisvert on Hummingbird Lane. Gregory Floyd claimed that his father had calmly tried to reason with Boisvert but that he had little success. "She [Boisvert] called him a murderer and a bald eagle," he told the judge. "She was trying to provoke my dad to have another heart attack." The younger Floyd also claimed it was the woman who was armed, not his father. "I could see the outline of a gun in her sweater," he alleged. "Ever since May [the Liko Kenney–McKay shooting] I've been in fear of guns." Robert Gainor, the chief prosecutor for the New Hampshire Department of Public Safety, poked a large hole in Gregory Floyd's testimony by pointing out that Floyd had made no mention of a gun during the initial call to police.

Michelle Floyd later testified that she too believed Alma Jean Floyd was packing a gun. Floyd's wife made her way to the witness stand with a noticeable limp and blinked repeatedly owing to her brain injury. She wore a flannel shirt, no makeup, and had her long brown hair tied back in a ponytail. Mrs. Floyd said she had been married to her husband for twenty-five years and did her best to paint him as the victim in this case. She also claimed he wasn't the man portrayed as a wild vigilante by bloggers and supporters of Liko Kenney. "My husband didn't have a choice in that situation," she said referring to the shooting.

From my perspective, Michelle Floyd certainly proved to be a sympathetic figure on the witness stand, but I had a difficult time believing her husband was the "gentle man" that she had described. The most powerful testimony of the trial came from the alleged victim herself, Alma Jean Boisvert. Clutching her chest and wiping away tears, the five-foot-two Boisvert made her way past the rows of spectators with her head down—a deliberate attempt to avoid eye contact with the defendant, who was clearly trying to rattle her with his cold, blank stare. Boisvert's voice cracked as she gave her name to the court.

"Are you nervous?" the prosecutor asked.

"A lot nervous," she replied. Boisvert explained that she cared for fifteen cats in her home. "I take them in when they're about to be put down." She and her husband had been staying at a time-share they owned in nearby Lincoln, New Hampshire, and she had only returned to Hummingbird Lane to provide medicine for a sick pet. She cared for the cat and was on her way back down Hummingbird Lane when she found her vehicle grill to grill with Floyd's pickup on the narrow, snow-covered road. "We're gonna be here all day, bitch!" Floyd allegedly barked at her. "What're you gonna do about it? You don't have rights. You've got a New Hampshire education. You don't know anything. I could just push you off the road!"

Alma Jean Boisvert returned to her 1996 Lincoln Town Car as Floyd continued to spew venom from his pickup truck. *Do you want me to pull a gun on you?* The threat kept ringing in her ears. The woman knew what Greg Floyd was capable of. She had read all about it in the newspapers and had seen it on television. "I didn't move," she told the court. "I didn't get out of the vehicle. That comment about the gun scared the beejeebees out of me." Boisvert said she was too scared to turn her back or to leave her car. Gregory Paul Floyd then jumped out of the truck and ran home to get his mother, who arrived at the scene moments later. Michelle Floyd quickly reminded Boisvert that she and her husband were disabled. "We're all handicapped," Michelle allegedly said. "We'll take you to federal court if he has a heart attack."

"Well," Boisvert replied. "He doesn't have a problem getting out and yelling at me!" Boisvert claims that Michelle Floyd responded by saying, "Who's gonna believe you? It's three against one." Floyd's wife did eventually break the stalemate by backing up her husband's pickup truck and allowing Alma Jean Boisvert to drive away. The woman said she tried to go to work that evening at a gift shop in North Woodstock but found herself crippled by fear. "I couldn't stop shaking. I couldn't stop crying." When asked by the prosecutor if she was still afraid of Greg Floyd, Boisvert admitted she was. "I knew he meant it," she said referring to the gun threat. "In my mind, in my heart."

The trial broke for a quick recess in late afternoon. Some observers sneaked out for a cigarette break, while reporters placed calls to their editors to brief them of the goings-on thus far. I made a visit to the bathroom, which was conveniently located across the hall from the courtroom. Like the courthouse itself, the bathroom was old and had not been updated with any of the modern conveniences like hands-free wash or flush. The bathroom had a few porcelain sinks and a few stalls. It was certainly quiet, though, at least when I entered. I was alone and I chose a stall furthest from the door and closest to the window. I locked the door behind me, sat down and began reviewing my notes. I didn't buy Greg Floyd's story and I doubted the judge did either. Alma Jean Boisvert's explanation of what had happened on Hummingbird Lane seemed much more consistent with the Greg Floyd I had begun to know from his statements in the Liko Kenney–McKay case. As I pondered this thought, I heard the creak of the bathroom door as it opened wide. I was alone no more. *Wouldn't it be interesting if I came outta this stall and saw Greg Floyd standing there?* I thought to myself. *It would certainly be a chance to hear his side of the story.* I folded my notebook, exited the stall, and could hardly believe my eyes. Greg Floyd was in the bathroom and it was now just the two of us. I walked slowly to the sink and turned the hot water on to wash my hands. Floyd was no longer the barrel-chested, bearlike figure I remembered from the police photographs. He was at least sixty pounds lighter now, but to me he was no less dangerous. He unnerved me greatly but I could not let him know it. "If you want to tell me your story, I'd love to hear it."

My invitation set his eyes ablaze. "Wanna tip?" he asked, drilling his index finger into my shoulder. "She's a fucking liar," he hissed through a mouth of rotting teeth and gums blackened from diabetes. Floyd began to rail against Alma Jean Boisvert and her family. "The police are covering up for them," he said, shaking his fist. "A man has no rights in this cocksucking state! Fuck her, fuck the judge, and fuck you!"

I could do nothing but stand my ground. "Can I quote you on that?" Floyd reached for his cane and for a moment I thought he would swing it toward my head. I raised my forearm in a defensive posture and prayed I would be strong enough to block the blow. Instead of launching into an attack, Floyd pivoted on his left foot and walked swiftly out of the bathroom. I opened my eyes and let out a deep breath. As Greg Floyd strolled away, I saw that he did so without any noticeable pain, discomfort, or limp.

When we returned to the courtroom Floyd was no longer interested in me. His eyes were focused now on Judge John P. Cyr, who was about to announce the verdict. *Hold on tight*, I said to myself. *This isn't gonna be good.*

"I find the defendant, Gregory Floyd, guilty," the judge announced, as a cheer erupted in the courtroom. "I order Mr. Floyd to serve twelve months in the Grafton County House of Correction."

Cyr continued to read his verdict with a mention of six months to serve and six suspended. I paid no attention to the judge's words as I zeroed in on the defendant, who had begun cursing in a quiet but deliberate voice. "Son of a bitch, know what the Constitution is?" he asked the judge. Floyd's lawyer told him to quiet down but this caused the man to scream louder. He swore at his defense attorney, which signaled the court officers over. "Fucking bastards," he hollered, while being led down the aisle in the center of the courtroom. The spectators all stood, watching the ex-Marine devolve into a raving madman. "Got something to say, fuckhead?" Floyd asked one Kenney supporter as he was being ushered away. Once again, Floyd was walking with purpose and the cane appeared to be nothing more than a prop. He reached the back of the courtroom and threw open the doors violently with both arms; the *boom!* reverberated through the building.

I grabbed my camera and followed the other reporters out into the hallway, where Floyd was now nose to nose with recently retired State Trooper Bret Beausoleil, who had testified in the trial. "You're not a goddamned cop," Floyd shouted, the spittle hanging from his lower lip. Beausoleil, who was the same height but much bulkier than Floyd, didn't move; in fact, he stood there with a slight grin on his face. Chris King then jumped to the front of the crowd and photographed Floyd with his digital camera. "What are you doing, *boy?*" Floyd yelled. A court officer grabbed Floyd by the arms and tried to usher him toward the elevator but the ex-Marine struggled to break free. "You goddamned people need to learn that America has the goddamned Constitution," Floyd shouted, while waving his cane like a sword around the hallway. Several more court officers grabbed the man and dragged him toward the elevator, pinning him against the door as he continued to yell.

"You murdered Liko Kenney, too," Chris King said, loud enough for Floyd to hear. "You murdered Liko Kenney, bro!"

The elevator door opened and Greg Floyd was shoved inside. The rest of us took off in a sprint down the stairs. "Where are they bringing him out?" I asked one reporter. "The basement," she replied, as the traveling media circus poured out of the building to the front steps of the courthouse. We heard a loud commotion coming from the right corner of the building and followed the sound, arriving seconds later to see Greg Floyd handcuffed and stuffed into a police car for the long ride to county jail. "I would never help a police officer again," Floyd told Captain Paul Leavitt of the Grafton County Sheriff's Department. "The next time I see someone lying in the road, I'll run over him myself!" Floyd's threats were muffled as officers slammed the back seat of the police car closed. I stood at the curb as the vehicle pulled away from the courthouse. Greg Floyd gazed angrily at the crowd of onlookers, some of whom were applauding as the car drove away.

"I hope they lock him up for good," Bill Kenney said, as I drove him back to the Tamarack Tennis Camp that afternoon. "But I know that won't happen. He'll be free again and then who knows what he'll do?" It was a question that I had asked myself after witnessing Floyd's violent explosion. Did he have the potential to become another Carl Drega? Would he feel pressure enough to lash out against his so-called enemies in a deadly way? I felt sorry for the townspeople, who would now be forced to look over their shoulder every day, praying the volcano that was Greg Floyd would not erupt. I returned to the Kinsman Lodge to review my notes once more, notes I had scribbled furiously while the drama unfolded around me. The only noise I heard now was Floyd's voice still ringing in my ears. The lodge was empty and quiet. Sue and Chet Thompson were vacationing in Florida, but had left me a key. Having the run of the old place, I walked up the creaky staircase and chose the biggest little bedroom I could find. Still in my clothes, I collapsed on the bed and slept for about an hour before I was awakened by the roar of my growling stomach. My caloric intake that day had consisted of two cups of coffee and a stale bagel. I needed a good meal and, more important, a good beer, so I got in my Volkswagon Jetta and headed for the Dutch Treat.

When I arrived at the bar, many of the faces I had seen at the courthouse were now huddled around a table, hoisting celebratory toasts to each other and to the memory of Liko Kenney. Chris King had a cell phone glued to his ear while being congratulated by well-wishers as if he had prosecuted the case against Greg Floyd himself. "Now we'll see if [Kelly] Ayotte has the guts to reopen Liko's case," King said gleefully. I was asked to join King's table and did so; however, I did not share in the merriment of watching Floyd unravel at the courthouse. Greg Floyd had promised that he would take matters into his own hands if he felt that his rights had been denied him. *What must he be thinking right now, stewing in county jail?* Try as I might, I could not get the image of Carl Drega's charred property out of my mind. I ordered a Sam Adams and sipped it quietly, soaking in the conversation around me. There was plenty of talk about the need for state police to raid Floyd's property on Hummingbird Lane. As a convicted felon, Floyd is barred from owning firearms. "Who knows what kind of arsenal he's got out there?" one woman said. As I was getting up to leave, another member of the group pulled me aside. "Wanna take a ride?" private investigator Brad Whipple asked. "Where to?" I countered.

"Can't tell you that," Whipple explained. "But I can tell you to bring your camera." I jumped into a car with Whipple and Chris King and drove back out onto Route 116 toward Easton. The sky over Franconia Notch had turned blood red as the last rays of sunlight dissolved slowly into darkness. Whipple flicked his headlights on while carefully navigating the minefield of frost heaves laid out on the road ahead of us. He slowed as we approached a storage facility on the righthand side of the road.

"What do we have here?" I asked.

Whipple looked at King and smiled: "We have the crime scene." He parked the car and fished for a key to open the storage garage. I climbed out of the back seat and immediately noticed a collection of large hoofprints in the snow. "Moose like to nose around here for some reason," Whipple sighed as he lifted the garage door. I took a step forward and then a step back, never taking my eyes off the object in front of me. It was a car, but not just any car. It was Liko Kenney's Toyota Celica and it was a truly haunting spectacle to behold.

"It looks just like it did the night of the shooting," Whipple told me. "Nothing's been changed." There was a small bullet hole at the top of the hood near the windshield. There was another small hole in the windshield itself surrounded by a small spider web of cracked glass. I walked over to the driver's-side window, which was open. I peered in and saw Liko Kenney's dried blood splattered across the headrest and back cushion of the driver's seat. The passenger seat, where Caleb Macaulay had been sitting, was covered with small shards of broken glass. There was a sheet of plastic draped over Liko's belongings in the back seat. I walked around the Celica quietly taking photographs, not saying a word. In fact, none of us spoke. It was as if we were all in fear of waking the dead. I had a sense that if Liko's spirit was anywhere, it was here inside his car and not buried six feet deep under a layer of cold ground at Tamarack.

"He didn't have to die," Chris King said, as much to himself as to Whipple and me. "Floyd murdered that boy plain and simple."

"What do you plan to do with this?" I asked.

"We'll use it as evidence at Floyd's murder trial," Whipple replied confidently. "The state has got to view Greg Floyd differently now."

In the following days, New Hampshire attorney general Kelly Ayotte announced there were no plans to reconsider criminal charges against Greg Floyd in the shooting death of Liko Kenney. "If new evidence came forward about the actual incident itself, we always have the ability to look at the case," she added. Ayotte said that up until this point, no one had presented any new evidence to sway her from her belief that Greg Floyd was a Good Samaritan and not a cold-blooded killer. One could argue that the evidence to warrant such an investigation against Floyd had been there from the very beginning. Kelly Ayotte has been and will forever be roundly criticized for her rush to judgment regarding Greg Floyd. The attorney general painted herself in a corner in her apparent need to paint Floyd as a hero. Had Ayotte shown the proper patience in the case, she would have discovered quite early the serious questions surrounding Floyd's alleged heroic deed:

1 Greg Floyd's initial testimony that he never warned Liko Kenney before he fired the fatal shot. (This detail was corroborated by Kenney's passenger Caleb Macauley).

2 Floyd's bizarre behavior and statements following the shooting. The ex-Marine told police and witnesses that he had killed between twenty and forty-three people for the government. Was Floyd simply lying to inflate his own ego? Or was he under the hallucinogenic effects of Serotonin Syndrome? "Sir, you can't shoot me, you'll be charged with murder," Caleb Macaulay told Floyd at the scene. "I'm on medication so it won't matter," Floyd allegedly replied.

3 Greg Floyd's penchant for violent behavior had been well established by police before the May 11, 2007, shooting.

There was no question in my mind that Greg Floyd's actions in the Liko Kenney–McKay case should have been examined more closely. As I returned to Boston, I couldn't help wondering how Ayotte's decision would play among the people of Franconia. I knew it would deflate the likes of Bill Kenney, Chris King, and Brad Whipple. While Floyd remained held on $20,000 cash bail, prosecutors filed a motion to send him to prison for parole violation. His 1998 conviction for assaulting a police officer had come with a one- to three-year prison sentence that was suspended for ten years as long as he remained on "good behavior." Terrorizing Alma Jean Boisvert did *not* constitute good behavior in the eyes of prosecutors. Despite their efforts, Greg Floyd was released from jail on June 16, 2008, on $80,000 personal recognizance bail. "Mr. Floyd's actions [in the Liko Kenney–McKay case] prove he is not someone who runs away," said his new, court-appointed lawyer, Simon Mayo, during the bail hearing. As a condition for bail, Floyd was ordered to relinquish any firearms, destructive devices, and ammunition. He was also ordered to stay away from anyone on the state's witness list—which, of course, included Alma Jean Boisvert. This stipulation provided little comfort for the woman who collapsed and was hospitalized at the mere idea that Floyd would be released. On December 27, 2008, supporters of Liko Kenney received a late Christmas present: prosecutors in Grafton County announced they would proceed with three cases against the ex-Marine. The announcement came after a sentencing deal that would have covered Floyd's conviction for threatening, the courtroom outburst that followed, and a reevaluation of the suspended sentence he had received more than ten years earlier for assaulting a state trooper. In March 2009, Grafton County Superior Court Judge Peter Bornstein ruled that Floyd's criminal threatening conviction was a violation of his parole. The judge sentenced the ex-Marine to one to three years in state prison.

15

He who does not prevent a
crime when he can encourages it.
SENECA

It was early autumn in Franconia Notch and more than a year since the tragedy on Route 116. The lightly sweet scents of the lupines were a distant memory now. I had journeyed back to Franconia for the sole purpose of interviewing Caleb Macaulay. I was hopeful that he would be willing to reflect more deeply about the shooting now that he had the benefit of both time and space. Don Merrill, owner of Merrill's Agway, had been serving as our go-between. He had been looking after the fragile young man and I felt their relationship went much deeper than that of owner and employee: Merrill treated Macaulay like a son. It had taken me months to gain Merrill's confidence about this project. Fortunately, he too felt the need for a historical account of what had happened on May 11, 2007. The deadly showdown had been a singular, explosive event that forever changed the way people in the North Country viewed themselves and one another. Only three living people—Caleb Macaulay, Greg Floyd, and Floyd's son—knew exactly what had happened on that fateful day, and their conflicting statements suggested at least one of them was not telling the full truth. During our many telephone conversations, Don Merrill had explained that Caleb wanted to meet me and get a feel for who I was and what I was setting out to do before he committed to saying anything on the record. Several times, Caleb had agreed to a meeting with me, but always backed out at the last minute.

"I want Caleb to be comfortable," I explained to Don Merrill. "We can do this anywhere and at any time he wants."

"Do you own a pair of hiking boots?" Merrill asked.

"Sure, I do," I replied in a curious tone.

"Caleb wants to take you on a hike around Franconia. He feels most comfortable when he's around nature."

I drove up to the North Country early one Sunday morning with my hiking boots and a backpack filled with bottled water, note-pads, and a tape recorder. I was told Caleb would call me on my cell phone to inform me exactly where we were supposed to meet. I arrived in Franconia just after 10 A.M. and drove along Route 116/Easton Road until I found a place to pull over. I sat in my car going over a mental checklist of questions I had planned to ask—questions I was not sure Caleb would be willing to answer. Most of all, I wanted Caleb to bring me back to that late afternoon when he went from being a quiet, carefree young man to becoming the key witness to one of the most shocking crimes in New England history. My cell phone rang at around 11 A.M. I answered and was surprised to hear the voice of Don Merrill and not Caleb Macaulay on the other end. "He's not coming," Merrill said softly.

"What do you mean he's not coming?" I asked, with a little agitation in my voice. "I've driven more than a hundred miles for this." My statement probably sounded hollow to Merrill. The has-sle of a morning drive from Boston to Franconia was nothing com-pared to what Caleb had been going through.

"He's just not ready," Merrill said. "I'm not sure he will ever be."

I asked Merrill to try to persuade Caleb once more to meet me but the Agway owner would not budge. I hung up the phone and swore, "Shit, what a wasted day this is." For a journalist, there is no worse feeling than when an interview falls through. I stepped out of my car to stretch my legs and heard the distant roar of the Ham Branch of the Gale River flowing nearby. As I continued feeling sorry for myself, it suddenly dawned on me why Caleb Macaulay pulled out of the meeting. "He never really got out of that Toy-ota," I whispered to myself. "A piece of his mind is still there, paralyzed by fear, sitting next to his friend's blood-soaked body and staring into the barrel of Greg Floyd's gun."

Caleb Macaulay was an innocent bystander who was now imprisoned by his own fear. This was a life sentence, in my estimation. I agreed with Merrill's belief that Caleb may never be mentally prepared enough to confront his past. I walked down to the river's edge and watched the torrent of water churning its way over and around large boulders and small rocks scattered along the river bed. It became a symbol to me of what this case—and what these men—were all about. The violent collision of water against rock represented the clash between the free-flowing Liko Kenney and the immovable object Bruce McKay. The clash was one of personalities and ways of life. For decades, descendants of Franconia's frontiersmen had been forced to live side by side with hippies—all enjoying the liberties and freedoms found in this small nirvana in northern New England.

Freedom, however, means different things to different people. To those townsfolk whose families can be traced back several generations in Franconia, freedom comes in the opportunity to create better lives for themselves and their children through hard work and a healthy respect for the structure and laws that govern them. Franconia's hippies view freedom in its purest form. They try to live free of societal mores and authority; natural law is the only law worth obeying. One could suggest that Liko Kenney and the hippies of Franconia enjoyed a sense of freedom that a hard-nosed officer like Bruce McKay could only dream about. The officer's only taste of true liberty came while riding his motorcycle through the mountains and hills around his home. Liko was not bound by the constraints and responsibilities of a family, a career, or a sense of duty; instead, he was free to roam around his own "sovereign nation." Bruce McKay and those like him understood that true individual freedom may have been a high ideal but it was also pure fantasy. To them, laws were put in place to prevent a communal breakdown from happening. Yet it was not the interpretation but the enforcement of those laws that triggered the greatest debate. A chasm between those on the side of law enforcement and those on the side of personal freedom still exists in Franconia. Many residents continue to hold a deep distrust of the police department and its chief—who, they believe, gave officers like McKay carte blanche to trample on their constitutional rights. And many area police officers with whom I have spoken are contemptuous of certain elements of the citizenry who show little respect for the law. These officers have refused to go on the record, fearing their words could be used as ammunition in the Kenney family's lawsuit against the town.

Among Liko Kenney supporters the tragedy is now referred to as "5/11." A silk-screen image of Liko with his fist raised appears on posters and bumper stickers across Franconia, where he is treated as a martyr by some. Liko Kenney has become a symbol of rebellion and freedom now. But, had Liko Kenney lived, would he still have enjoyed the same legion of support? Or would he be left alone to count his last days on death row, like fellow cop killer Michael "Styx" Addison? When fighting for a conviction in the Addison trial, prosecuting attorney Will Delker argued that although the shooting had not been planned out, it was most certainly intentional: "He [Addison] chose to have that gun with him. He chose to reassemble it. He chose to load it. He chose to pull it out of his pants. He chose to point it at Officer Briggs, and he chose to pull the trigger." Hadn't Liko Kenney made similar choices to ensure equally grave results? One could argue that Liko Kenney's crime was even more egregious: he not only shot Corporal McKay but then proceeded to strike him with his Toyota Celica—twice! Liko's family insists that he should have been afforded a trial for his crime instead of being gunned down by Greg Floyd. There is little doubt that previous allegations of aggressive policing by Bruce McKay would have come to light if such a trial did take place. But how would a jury have responded to the heart-wrenching words of Sharon Davis-McKay or an orphaned Courtney McKay about their shared sense of loss? Would Liko's supporters still view him as a small-town version of Che Guevara, the handsome Marxist guerrilla fighter whose own admirers have stubbornly overlooked his murderous deeds?

The romantic image of Liko Kenney is lost on Bruce McKay's loved ones. Sharon Davis-McKay doesn't need a bumper sticker to remember her fiancé. Bruce remains alive in her mind and at the summit of Cannon Mountain where the two were to be married. After he was cremated, Sharon took some of his ashes there, scattered them, and said goodbye. She now helps support others who have lost loved ones in the line of duty. In May 2008, a year after the shootings, Sharon Davis-McKay traveled to Washington, D.C., to see her fiancé's name added to the National Law Enforcement Memorial, where etched across white marble walls are the names of more than 17,500 men and women. Franconians may never understand the man Bruce McKay was, but those who walk along these "pathways of remembrance," under the watchful eye of a cast-iron lion protecting its cubs, recognize the sacrifice made by all officers killed in the line of duty.

A legacy of remembrance is also under way in Franconia for the Old Man of the Mountain, which had kept a watchful eye over the notch for ten thousand years before it came crashing down during a spring storm. Like the Old Man's demise, there is a sense of both randomness and inevitability in the shooting deaths of Bruce McKay and Liko Kenney. The tragedy was seemingly random in that both men along with Greg Floyd were thrown together in a perfect storm of violence that terrible day. Liko Kenney just happened to be returning home from Agway with a pistol in his car; Bruce McKay just happened to forget to wear his protective vest when he went out patrolling Route 116; and Greg Floyd just happened to be on his way home from a trip to the market with a dangerous combination of prescription drugs in his system.

Conspiracy theorists may balk at this notion. There are those who believe that McKay was targeting Kenney with the assistance of Greg Floyd. Beth Towle Kenney is among those who feel McKay was zeroing in on her nephew that day. She claims to have passed McKay's squad car minutes earlier while traveling at a high rate of speed. "Why didn't he stop me?" she asks. "Why did he insist on stopping Liko for an expired registration?" It's a question that could only have been answered by McKay himself. There is little doubt that the officer held a grudge against the unbridled young man not only for grabbing and twisting his manhood but also because Liko Kenney was everything Bruce McKay was not. Liko was a member of Franconia's most famous family and probably felt a sense of entitlement that caused him to look down on authority. I had not witnessed this attitude from any of the Kenney family members I had spoken to but I understand there are others who felt that way about them. Growing up on Cape Cod, I had witnessed a similar entitled manner among some members of the Kennedy clan, who treated townsfolk as merely an extension of their household staff.

What Bruce McKay could not have realized, however, was that Liko's burdens originated from within. His learning disabilities had handcuffed his intellectual growth and his prospects were slim in New Hampshire, despite an unemployment rate that was much lower than the national average. Liko had seen his sister Mahina go off to college, but where could he go without even a high school diploma? The military was out of the question. Despite his grandfather Jack Kenney's service in World War II, the conflicts in Vietnam and Iraq had turned the Kenney clan against the military. Liko Kenney would stay behind to fight the battle of Franconia Notch instead. His dream of moving to Oregon to raise cattle was just that—a dream. Liko barely made enough money working at Merrill's Agway to feed himself, let alone save for a move cross-country. Jo Miller had visited her nephew shortly before he was killed. She brought over some pizza because Liko and his friends were once again short on cash. "I listened to these young men talk about the lack of opportunity in Franconia," Miller remembers. "These guys were in a hole and I was saddened because they had no idea how to dig themselves out." It was a hole dug by Liko's own hands. "He just wasn't motivated to achieve on that kind of level," his father Davey admits. "His sister was a real go-getter from the very beginning. She had a real confident aura about her. Liko never had that."

The showdown was random yet it seems that everyone in the small community—including Liko Kenney—knew it was going to happen eventually. The young man's sense of dread could be felt by all of those around him. He had written about it in his journal and had predicted his own demise in eerie detail to the father of a dead friend. There is a shared sense of guilt from townsfolk who witnessed the warning signs but never had the courage to speak up and attempt to diffuse the growing volatility of the situation. The deaths of Kenney and McKay were the tragic result of a confluence of events that had begun in 2003 on that snowy evening at Fox Hill Park. Liko Kenney and Bruce McKay had been on a collision course for years afterward, evoking the aura of the Old West: the town just wasn't big enough for the two of them. Fate then added Greg Floyd to the mix and the outcome was inevitable. There is a strong chance that the bloodshed could have even been worse had Caleb Macaulay not had the presense of mind to refuse Floyd's order to pick up Liko's gun.

The deadly confrontation mirrors the downfall of the Old Man of the Mountain, not only in its randomness and inevitability but also in the impact it has left on those around it. Those fortunate enough to have gazed upon the Old Man of the Mountain will tell you that the image of the gigantic rock formation appeared to change depending upon where you were standing. From a certain vantage point, the Great Stone Face looked like nothing more than an odd collection of rocks protruding from the side of Cannon Mountain; from another view, one could see the unmistakable outline of a human face, "a work of Nature in her mood of majestic playfulness." Like the Old Man, one's perception of Bruce McKay, Liko Kenney, and even Greg Floyd differs greatly depending upon where one stands in this case. William Shakespeare once wrote, "Time is the justice that examines all offenders," and this tragedy will be debated in the North Country for generations to come. The trials for all three men will take place at kitchen tables, in online chat rooms and in the corner booths of neighborhood bars. The sons and daughters of law enforcement officers may continue to remember Corporal Bruce McKay as a loving father and fallen hero, while the next generation of hippies will likely view Liko Kenney as a bright young man, a fellow searcher for the Age of Aquarius, who was forced to kill, only to be himself cut down by gunfire. Greg Floyd also has his supporters, especially among the family of Bruce McKay. The slain officer's father and his sister Meggen visited Floyd shortly after the shooting at his home on Hummingbird Lane. The McKays found Greg Floyd to be nothing like the man who had confronted me at the Littleton District Courthouse. The McKays described Greg Floyd as thoughtful, introspective, and above all humbled by his actions on the evening of May 11, 2007. There is truth in the descriptions of all three men, just as there is a darker reality.

As I left the bank of the Gale River and returned to my car I understood that I wouldn't get to meet Caleb Macaulay face-to-face but I felt that I had nonetheless gained a new perspective of the case. There was a chill in the air; in about a month's time, Franconia would be covered by a blanket of fresh snow. Before heading back to the highway toward Boston, I stopped by the Franconia Village Store to grab a cup of coffee for the road. I placed my order and glanced at the collection of press clippings about Bode Miller that lined the walls. The town clearly wanted to be known for its connection to a favorite son and not for the crimes of his troubled cousin. "Think you'll get a lot of snow this winter?" I asked the clerk, as she poured hot coffee into my cup.

"We've seen more than our share of bad storms around here," she replied.

"I know you have," I muttered to myself. "I know."

AUTHOR'S NOTE

This book is not only the result of this writer's research and theories, but the cumulative effort of a community of people that recognized the need for an unbiased historical account of the events of May 11, 2007. I could not have completed this challenge without their assistance. I also could not have performed this task without the incredible work of journalists from the *Union Leader*, the *Concord Monitor*, and the *Caledonian-Record*. My goal was to separate the unfiltered reality from the perceptions clouded by passions on all sides of this case. I thank my editor Richard Pult for pushing me to examine not only the shooting itself, but the broader impact such a tragic event had on the people of New Hampshire.

I also thank Davey and Michele Kenney for sharing memories of their son. Thanks also to Bill Kenney, Mike Kenney, and Jo Miller for opening up about Liko. By the same token, I am eternally grateful to Sharon Davis-McKay, Meggen Payerle, and N. Bruce McKay for allowing their personal stories to be told. I also thank Chris King and Franconia Police Chief Mark Montminy for sharing documents and their opposing views on the case. To Brad Whipple—thanks for the tour into the heart of darkness.

To Sue and Chet Thompson—thanks for the great hospitality and the great breakfast. I cannot recommend the Kinsman Lodge enough to those who wish to experience the beauty of the North Country for themselves. To the folks at the Dutch Treat—thanks for the burger, the beer and the colorful conversation. To Don Merrill—thanks for the help and thanks for watching over Caleb. To Rhode Island state trooper Marc Lidsky—thanks for the professional insight. To Rob Hayward—sorry for your loss but thanks for the stories.

On the homefront there is no greater gift than the support I received from my wife, Laura, and my daughters, Isabella and Mia. Sorry daddy couldn't have taken you to the park more often while I was tackling this project. I love you! I also thank my mother, Diane Dodd, and her husband, Kenneth, as well as my brother, Todd Sherman, and my uncle, Jim Sherman.

I also thank once again the folks at Borders Express in Hanover, Massachusetts, for their unwavering support through the years. I also thank the following people for their support and for helping me reach a greater audience; Howie Carr, Dan Rea, Gerry Callahan, John Dennis, Jon Keller, Liz Walker, Donna Greer, Dana Barbuto, Gayle Fee, Laura Raposa, Mark Schmidt from the Winslow House, Frank and Denise Judge, Peter and Lixian Barry, John and Colleen Somers, Keith and Zoe Schofield, Herb and Toby Duane, David Robichaud, Jessi Miller, Kasey Kaufman, Debbi Kim, Eileen Curran, and of course the bus stop gang.

BIBLIOGRAPHY

Law Enforcement Agency Reports

Report of The Attorney General Concering the Deaths of
Franconia Police Corporal Bruce McKay and Liko Kenney
on May 11, 2007, in Franconia, New Hampshire

Officer Safety Notice
Subject Liko Kenney Date of Notice 04/25/07 Cpl. Bruce McKay
    Reporting

New Hampshire State Police Continuation of Investigation Report
Case No. MC-07-4121
Sgt. Michael Marshall interview with Caleb Macauley, May 11, 2007
Trooper G.M. Hildreth 11 May 2007 Contact with Caleb Macauley

New Hampshire State Police Continuation of Investigation Report
Case No. MC-07-4121
Sergeant Charles West interview with Gregory Willis Floyd, May 11, 2007
Trooper Michael J. Kokoski and Detective Russell Hubbard interviews with
    Gregory Paul Floyd, May 11, 2007

Division of State Police Continuation of Investigation Report
Case No. MC-07-4121
Sgt. M.C. Armaganian interview with Sgt. David Wentworth, May 12, 2007
Statement of Trooper Nathan B. Hamilton, May 12, 2007
Narrative for Patrolman Phillip R. Blanchard, May 12, 2007
Trooper Michael J. Kokoski On-Scene Activity/Observations, May 12, 2007

New Hampshire State Police Continuation of Investigation Report
Case No. MC-07-4121
TFC William J. Cantwell III interview with Susan Thompson, May 12, 2007
Statement of Susan M. Thompson
TFC William J. Cantwell III interview of Rebecca Thompson-Bell, May 12,
    2007

New Hampshire State Police Continuation of Investigation Report
Case No. MCU-07-1421
Trooper Michael J. Kokoski interview with Stanley and Brandon Sherburn,
    May 11, 2007

Sgt. M. A. Macfadzen interview with Charles Herbert, May 12, 2007

Trooper Seth E. Cooper interview with Nancy Van Kleek, Rebecca T. Bell, and Chester Thompson, May 11, 2007

TFC Peter Todd interview with William Tucker Scheffer, Alison Morris, and Richard G. Morris, May 12, 2007

Sgt. Paul Hunt interview with Sam Stephenson, May 11, 2007

Statements from Steven Czarnecki, Floraine L. Robinson-Place, Evelyn L. Eastton, and Amy Cyrs, May 13, 2007

Trooper Michael J. Kokoski interview with Allan Clark, May 13, 2007

Statement from Allan Clark, May 11, 2007

Trooper Russell E. Hubbard interview with Cindy A. Carpinetti, May 15, 2007

New Hampshire State Police Continuation of Investigation Report
Case No. MC-07-1421

List of items recovered from body of Norman Bruce McKay transferred from Trooper Michael Cote to Sgt. Robert Bruno, June 7, 2007

Written Overview of Easton Road, (Route 116) Franconia, New Hampshire

Transcipts between Dispatcher and 44K (Bruce McKay) and Dispatcher and Gregory Floyd

Video Works DV Tape (McKay-Kenney, May 11, 2007)

New Hampshire Case No. MC-07-4121

Sgt. Michael Marshall interview with Don Merrill, May 14, 2007

Sgt. Michael Marshall interview with Suzanne Merrill, May 14, 2007

New Hampshire Case No. MC-07-4121

Trooper Michael Kokowski interview with Dave Clark, June 10, 2007

New Hampshire Case No. MC-07-4121

Trooper Nathan B. Hamilton interview with Chris Fowler, May 19, 2007

New Hampshire Case No. MC-07-4121

Sgt. Charles West interview with Scott J. Walker, June 6, 2007

New Hampshire Case No. MCU-07-4121

Trooper Michael Kokowski interview with Steven Dunleavey, June 10, 2007

New Hampshire Case No. MCU-07-4121

Trooper Michael Kokowsky interview with Brenda Saunders, June 10, 2007

New Hampshire Case No. MC-07-4121

Trooper Nathan B. Hamilton interview with Matthew Chernicki, June 10, 2007

New Hampshire Case No. MC-07-4121

New Hampshire State Police Possessed Property Report—1984 Toyota Celica Coupe—Owner Liko Kenney

New Hampshire Case No. MC-07-4121
Trooper Sheldon Belanger—Written Overview of 1984 Toyota Celica

New Hampshire Case No. MC-07-4121
Sgt. Charles West—May 16, 2007 contact with ATF

Franconia Police Incident Report—01/29/2003, Fox Hill Park
Statement from N. B. McKay, Franconia Police Department
Statement from Sgt. Richard Ball, Bethlehem Police Department
Statement from Officer Steve Cox, Littleton Police Department
Evidence Examination Request (Tranportation/Possession of a Controlled
  Substance-Suspect Liko P. Kenney)
State of New Hampshire Complaints (Simple Assault, Obstructing
  Government Administration, Resisting Arrest of Detention, Escape, Acts
  Prohibited)

Office of Grafton County Attorney
Letter to Attorney Simon Brown about Timothy Stephenson's accounts of
  instances with Mr. Bruce McKay, June 24, 2004

New Hampshire State Police Incident Report: F07-002882
Reckless Conduct; Place Another in Danger (Victim, Richard W. Larcom/
  Offender Liko P. Kenney)
Trooper Brian W. Doyle interview with Richard W. Larcom and Donna
  S. Larcom

New Hampshire State Police Incident/Arrest Report: F03-0055
Criminal Mischief Charge against Liko P. Kenney/Victim: Larisa
  Alexandrovna Kenney
Trooper Matthew Koehler interview with Larisa Kenney, January 16, 2003

New Hampshire State Police Incident/Arrest Report: F-070279
Burglary/Theft By Taking (Victim: Liko Kenney/Offender: Juvenile)
Sergeant Robert E. Bruno interview with suspects, January 29, 2007
Sergeant Bret Beausoleil contact with Liko Kenney, February 5, 2007
Sergeant Bret Beausoleil investigation of Witness Tampering against Liko
  P. Kenney, April 25, 2007

State of New Hampshire Complaint Docket #80570C
Criminal Threatening complaint against Gregory W. Floyd, January 8, 2008

New Hampshire State Police Criminal Investigation Case #97-1006
Criminal Threatening complaint against Gregory W. Floyd, June 22, 1998
TFC Robert E. Bruno interview with Trooper Russell Hubbard regarding
  Gregory W. Floyd
Easton, NH Police Chief Robert Every narrative of Gregory W. Floyd,
  May 19, 1997

Affidavit in Support of Search Warrant (Robert Every)
Trooper Scot E. Bryan interview with Shay Littlefield, June 16, 1997
TFC Robert E. Bruno Arrest Warrant for Gregory W. Floyd, July 23, 1997

Newspapers

"Bill honoring Bruce McKay divisive." *Concord Monitor*, January 17, 2008.
"Complaints: Officer was aggressive." *Concord Monitor*, August 15, 2007.
"Even in tragedy, we must ask." *Concord Monitor*, May 20, 2007.
"Fallen officer deserves to be memorialized." *Concord Monitor*, January 15, 2007.
"Floyd Released from County Jail." *Caledonian-Record*, June 17, 2008.
"Franconia Recovery Committee Conducting Survey on Tragedy." *Caledonian-Record*, June 23, 2007.
"Friends recall 'dreamer' Kenney." *Union Leader*, May 21, 2007.
"Last respects for fallen officer." *Concord Monitor*, May 18, 2007.
"Man in middle of shooting was 'loner.'" *Concord Monitor*, May 14, 2007.
"McKay memorial put on hold." *Concord Monitor*, January 18, 2007.
"McKay remembered as both dedicated, complex." *Union Leader*, May 13, 2007.
"My dad was so much more than that." *Union Leader*, May 18, 2007.
"Officer, shooter had angry past." *Concord Monitor*, May 13, 2007.
"Officers accused of using sirens to get to funeral." *Union Leader*, June 6, 2008.
"Officers honored at state memorial." *Concord Monitor*, May 19, 2007.
"Passer-by's use of deadly force cleared by AG." *Concord Monitor*, May 13, 2007.
"Prosecutor: Exonerating Floyd was right call." *Union Leader*, January 20, 2008.
"Reconciliation the goal after a double slaying." *Concord Monitor*, July 17, 2007.
"Reports list McKay's use of force." *Concord Monitor*, July 26, 2007.
"Survey reveals a town in pain." *Union Leader*, July 17, 2007.
"This hit in the gut." *Union Leader*, August 19, 2007.
"Uncle says nephew was 'loose cannon.'" *Concord Monitor*, May 13, 2007.
"Video shows final moments." *Union Leader*, June 26, 2007.
"Working to help Franconia heal." *Union Leader*, May 31, 2007.

Books, Magazines, and Web sites

Heald, Bruce D. *The Franconia Gateway.* Charleston, S.C.: Arcadia. 2002.
Layden, Tim. Bode's Bumpy Trail. SI.com (accessed May 15, 2007).
Miller, Bode, with Jack McEnany. *Bode: Go Fast, Be Good, Have Fun.* New York: Villard Books, 2005.

Mudge, John T. B., comp. and ed. *The Old Man's Reader: History & Legends of Franconia Notch*. Etna, N.H.: Durand Press. 1995.

Poole, Ernest. *The Great White Hills of New Hampshire*. Illustrated by Garth Williams. Garden City, N.Y.: Doubleday, 1946.

Ramsey, Floyd W. *Shrouded Memories: True Stories from the White Mountains of New Hampshire*. Littleton, N.H.: Bondcliff Books, 2002.

Sedgwick, John. "Collision Course." *Boston Magazine* (May 15, 2007).